Slay the Dragon

NOT EACH OTHER

**Would you like to develop
the following skills and abilities?
If so, then this book is for you!**

• Uncover the hidden fear of feeling good and overcome the unconscious addiction to feeling bad: anxious, angry, depressed

• Become more *effective* in the face of stress & conflict

• Based on the mind-body link, do your part to have a healthy heart by replacing a fear focus with a love focus every time stress strikes

• Effectively handle being verbally attacked

• Transform conflicts at home or work from a battle of fear and anger into a dance of love

• Use road rage and other stresses as a vehicle for healing the hidden hurts of your past that interfere with present happiness

• Calmly handle your loved ones' (your children's and your love partner's) negative emotions

• Conquer your fear, depression, and anxiety

• Uncover and heal the source of an urge to hurt someone you love

• Be more effective in handling criticism at home and work

• Transform your anger, fear, sadness, and depression into love

• Learn how to listen when you're angry and feel like launching into a verbal attack and argument

Also by Dr. Stephen Royal Jackson

8 Steps to Love
*How to Return to Love When You
Need it the Most—the Moment
Stress & Conflict Begin*

A Matter of Love
*A Fascinating Journey About
Following and Fulfilling
Your Divine Destiny*

Love Conquers Stress
*Applying the 8 Steps to Love
to Various Kinds of Stress*

Love, Stress & Sex
*Applying the 8 Steps to Love
to the Stress of Love & Sex*

Words Become Flesh
*True Stories of How Words
Hidden in Your Heart Become
The Flesh of Your Life*

Slay the Dragon

NOT EACH OTHER

A Guide to Help You Vanquish the Inner
Source of Stress, Anxiety, Anger & Conflict

Stephen Royal Jackson, Ph.D.

Published by
SET Publishing
Wilmington, Delaware

For information address:
SET for Life Seminars, Inc.
2304 Riddle Avenue
Suite 406
Wilmington, Delaware 19806

Cataloging-in-Publication Data is available
from the Library of Congress
LCCN 2005937943
ISBN 978-1466335851

Dedicated to Janet and her mother Marjorie for teaching me by their triumph over tragedy that love truly does conquer stress, fear, and anger.

A Special Thank You to my agent Jaki Baskow for her unwavering faith in me and my message, and to Vanessa whose sweet soul came to me in a dream to prepare the way . . . I also wish to express my gratitude to the late Dr. Charles Stroebel for inspiring me with his research on stress . . .

CONTENTS

Dear Reader

YOU MAY ASK, "WHAT DO SUCH DIVERSE CONCEPTS AS DRAGONS, everyday violence, stress, love, anger, anxiety, and depression have to do with each other?" My response: everything.

In my clinical practice, I came to see how it is love that brings people into therapy. A lost relationship through death or divorce. A lack of self-love in the form of depression and low self-esteem. But deeper than these symptoms is the fact that at the core of our very being we are love. The capacity to love and care is our essence.

As such, you wouldn't be vulnerable to suffering from anger, anxiety, and depression if you didn't give a damn—if you didn't love and care. And because you do, you feel mad, glad, and sad.

The trick is how do you return to love when stress strikes and the fire of anger and anxiety begin to blaze, blackening the walls of your heart? Recent research has shown that anger, anxiety, and depression actually hurt the health of the heart. Negative emotions do violence to the heart by contributing to heart attacks.

Although this book can be considered a companion guide to *8 Steps to Love*, it can be read by itself. Should you decide to read *8 Steps to Love*, you will deepen your understanding and ability to master your negative emotions: anxiety and fear, anger and rage, sadness and depression. If you choose to read *A Matter of Love*, you will deepen your understanding of both the emotional and spiritual steps you can take in the face of stress and conflict. Should you decide to read *Words Become Flesh*, you'll discover how dramatically the words you use can affect your health. The words you say to yourself consciously, and those you repress in the form of intense emotions, can become the flesh of physical symptoms.

As I have said elsewhere, the 8 steps to love and the three techniques they contain are an outgrowth of three pillars of my experience: the athletic, the psychological, and the spiritual.

The athlete in me wanted to develop a way for people to move through life with the least amount of tension in response to the inevitable stress of life. The goal is to live life gracefully and smoothly like a great dancer or athlete. Pleasure becomes the norm, and stress becomes a momentary deviation. For so many, stress is the norm with no relief except on vacation.

The therapist in me wanted to develop a method of self-therapy and spiritual growth. In-depth therapy helps us resolve long-standing and repeated relationship stress. I wanted to provide steps for you to USE stress to achieve happiness in your life and relationships.

These steps are presented in a detailed and in-depth manner in *8 Steps to Love*. *Love Conquers Stress* shows you how to apply the steps to common kinds of stress, including the stress of conflict, road rage, death of a loved one, divorce, eating disorders, disease, aches, and pain, etcetera. *Love, Stress & Sex* shows you how to apply the steps to various sexual problems so you can liberate your love life.

The 8 steps are based on my heart-and-soul-centered-spiritual psychology. As such, the steps combine ancient healing wisdom and the therapeutic modalities of the four branches of modern psychology: behavioral therapy, cognitive therapy, psychodynamic (emotionally-expressive) therapy, and transpersonal therapy.

My mission in this book as in my other books remains the same: to help people find freedom from the needless suffering and senseless evil caused by ineffective ways of dealing with the stress and conflict of life. Both *A Matter of Love* and *Words Become Flesh* explore the psychodynamics of some of these senseless evils. However, unlike my other books, this book provides a sequential-skill-based program for mastering the steps that can help you be more *effective* in managing stress and conflict. The program is set up to be done in ten weeks: you focus on one chapter a week. However, it can be done at your own pace. It's up to you.

Stephen Royal Jackson, Ph.D.
November 29, 2005

There is no fear in love; but perfect love casteth out fear because fear hath torment. He that feareth is not perfect in love (1 John 4:18).

One has but to observe the world at large, to see what discord in thought and feeling does to the beautiful bodies that nature provides . . . Over the years, as one goes through life, the body becomes incapacitated . . . because the outer waking consciousness does not obey the One Law of Life—Love, Harmony, Peace!

—Saint Germain

My feelings are nothing to fear,
As they lead back to my heart,
To what's important and dear.

—from *8 Steps to Love*

As long as you are unaware of . . . your longing for . . . love from your parents and your resentment against them, you are bound to try remedying the situation in your later years . . . in your attempt to reproduce the childhood situation so as to correct it. . . . The most frequent way of attempting to remedy the situation is in your choice of love partners.

—Eva Pierrakos

Introduction

The Dragon Within

THE HIDDEN INNER SOURCE OF STRESS & CONFLICT

YOUR HAIR IS BRISTLING ON THE BACK OF YOUR NECK. You feel the heated flush of anger shoot up through your body. The urge to throw something seizes you. Perhaps you're on the phone with an annoying client, and you feel your muscles tensing and preparing to slam down the phone. If you are a mother or father you find yourself, almost without warning, ready to scream at your kids. What's going on?

The dragon in its physiological form as the reptile brain has been activated. This primitive portion of our brain is governed by the innate fight-or-flight response to stress. Either avenue is an attempt to survive. The reptile brain is geared to seek pleasure and to avoid pain. The sympathetic branch of the autonomic nervous system takes over. You are prepared to fight or flee from a perceived danger. Rapid, shallow chest breathing begins. Facial muscles tighten. Eye muscles tense and you focus your gaze into a fixed stare. Your large skeletal muscles tense up and the small, smooth muscles around your blood vessels constrict. You are ready for danger.

All this physiological arousal is fine if the threat is physical: you need to jump out of the way of a speeding truck. But most stress is emotional. You are stuck in traffic and are going to be late for work. Or you're having an argument with your spouse or kids.

Once the dragon in you has begun to sink its teeth and claws into

1

your heart, you constrict your heart, your feelings of love. You are angry, anxious, or depressed. On the one hand, you may feel like striking out verbally or physically. On the other hand, you may want to emotionally withdraw and give up or run away.

You know the scenarios. A potential for violence erupts. A mother hits her kids. A man attempts to hurt his wife. A soccer mom with a van full of kids screams at a man in his BMW: he just cut her off and made her swerve, endangering her young passengers.

In its drive to seek pleasure and avoid pain, the dragon within us sends us on the *outer quest* to find something external to us to relieve our stress: an argument, a cigarette, a drink, a piece of candy. To stop the dragon in its tracks, we must engage in the *inner quest*.

We must enter the dragon's cave of transformation: a symbol for the inner space we create by breathing slowly and deply. It is the *cocoon* where the clingy caterpillar becomes a butterfly. It is the alchemist's *laboratory* where the *lead* of our anger, fear, and depression becomes the *gold* of love. It is the *shell* of the oyster where, in the folds of soft-white tissue, a parasite is transformed into a pearl.

Overall Format for Mastering the Steps that Slay the Dragon

The dragon has four aspects: physical, mental, emotional, and spiritual. And we take physical, mental, emotional, and spiritual steps to slay the dragon. Nonetheless, even though each step has its particular emphasis, we address all four aspects of the dragon of our dependency and desire at once. That is to say, we find our physical, mental, emotional, and spiritual freedom from the core, implied belief of the dragon. In its most basic form it is *as if* we tell ourselves, "I AM dependent on something external to myself for relief from stress so that I can feel good and be at peace." Each step helps us cut through this belief and shows it to be an illusion. Besides being rooted in the reptile brain, this belief is reinforced by the prolonged physical dependency of our childhood and adolescence.

Each of the four inner steps helps you to feel good and be at peace in response to stress and conflict. Like a sword, each step cuts into the heart of the dragon by showing us we are *not* dependent on anything external to ourselves to feel good and be at peace.

How the Dragon Fuels the Stress of Conflict with Others

In conflicts with others, the enemy we need to attack is not them, it is the dragon within us. Unless we attack and slay the dragon's implied belief, we are at risk for throwing gas on the fire by trying to control others. We'll argue and fight *as if* we can't feel good and be at peace until the other person agrees with us, or until he or she feels better. It's as if we say, "I can't feel better until *you* do."

However, we make matters worse by acting as if we *need* them to feel good *before* we can feel good. This results in us being like runaway freight trains, riding roughshod over the negative feelings of others. We try to stifle their anger, fear, anxiety, depression, etcetera. Instead of helping them feel better, we make things worse by trying to force them to feel better by fighting and arguing. "You *shouldn't* feel bad about that. It's not worth getting upset over."

The other person feels forced to defend his or her feelings. But once we take responsibility for our own feelings, we can be more *effective* in helping the other person feel better. Once we have slain the dragon in a particular situation and we are feeling relaxed, we can then apply the four outer steps to effectively listen. With the four inner steps, we learn to relax first, and then proceed to deal coolly and calmly with the stress of conflict.

After we master the four inner steps for slaying the dragon, we focus on the four outer steps that keep the dragon from rearing its ugly head and wreaking havoc on our relationships. The four outer steps help us be more effective at managing conflict with others.

Doing a Daily Review of Your Progress in Slaying the Dragon

It will help you progress in developing the skills associated with each of the four inner and four outer steps if you keep a stress journal. Use a notebook or create a file on your personal computer. At the end of each day, keep a daily record of the situations that stressed you. It helps to organize your daily review in the following manner. You will dissect your reaction to help you become more aware. With greater awareness come freedom, peace, and control.

Format for Your Daily Review

1. Stressful Situation

Look back over your day, and ask yourself, "What were the situations in which I felt stressed? Angry (irritated, frustrated, annoyed, resentful, bitter)? Anxious (scared, nervous, jittery, afraid? Or depressed (sad, unhappy, defeated, deflated, down, blue).?" Use the questions below to *dissect* your reaction to one situation at a time.

2. Reaction

• **Images & Sensations:** What fantasies/pictures/images *flashed* through your mind? Did you *imagine* running away? Smashing things? Screaming? Hitting? Did your face feel hot and flushed? Did you lose your breath in fear? Did your chest muscles tighten? Did your jaw clench? What did you imagine?

• **Desires & Emotions:** What did you feel like saying or doing? What thoughts did you have?

• **Words & Actions:** What did you say or do? Anything you regret?

3. Steps (creative counter-actions): How did you apply any of the four inner or four steps to relieve your stress and conflict?

4. Replace & Resolve: What would you have loved to have said and done instead? Spell out the steps you would take. What would you say or do differently if you could do it all over again? Resolve to do this in similar situations in the future. As you imagine replacing your reaction, be sure to actually do slow-deep-belly breathing.

The following is a sample daily review. Frank is a thirty-five-year-old married man who was stressed by a call from his wife.

A Sample Daily Review

1. Stressful Situation

My wife calls me at work to complain about her mother. I listen to her upset over her mother criticizing her for buying too much food. After five minutes, I ask her why she went grocery shopping when she knows her mother is going to visit. "You know your mother stops by every Tuesday afternoon. And you know that she is always on you to be more frugal. She has that 1930's Depression mentality," I remind her. To which, she shouts, "It's enough I have to take her sh-t, but I have to hear your sh-t on top of hers."

2. Reaction

- **Images & Sensations:** A fantasy of myself smashing the phone down flashed through my mind. I saw the plastic phone shatter. I instantly felt a hot rush of sensations in my chest.
- **Desires & Emotions:** I felt enraged, and I thought: *What I have to say isn't sh-t! I have damn good ideas!*
- **Words & Actions:** I groaned out a growling sound as I clenched my teeth. No words. And I squeezed and raised the phone preparing to slam it down.

3. Steps (creative counter-actions): None. But, I am glad that I did not smash the phone.

4. Replace & Resolve: If I could do it all over again, I would stop myself before I gritted my teeth, groaned, growled, and started to slam the phone down. I would silently shout, "STOP!" I would then breathe in and think c-o-o-l. And then I'd breathe out, and think c-a-l-m. In similar situations in the future I resolve to stop myself from losing my cool. I will respond coolly and calmly.

(**Note:** Remember that faithfully practicing the daily review will accelerate your progress in mastering the steps for slaying the dragon and transforming your life and relationships.)

Important Instructions for Getting the Most Out of this Book

There are different skills to practice with each step. You can do this on a week-by-week basis, or at your own pace. Just be sure to stay with working on one skill at a time until you feel ready to move on.

Work one chapter per week. At the start of each week, be sure to read through each chapter in one sitting, and practice the skills in that chapter. Then, throughout your day as stress strikes, practice the skills you are working on for that week. At the end of each day, set aside a few minutes to do your daily review.

You may want to go through the book with a partner: your spouse or a friend. If you are doing this with another person, you can do your daily review aloud. You each take a turn practicing the step detailed in one chapter at a time. You take turns reviewing each stressful situation one at a time. The person sharing his or her list of stressful situations from the day also reviews what he or she would do to counter the stress. The person tells and demonstrates how he or she would apply the skills in the chapter.

At first, the steps may seem awkward, mechanical, and they may appear to be a lot to learn. For the sake of mastering the steps, we break them down into their separate components. With practice, the steps become a fluid process that can happen in just seconds. The goal is for the steps to be a new set of healthy habits.

The dragon's habitual ways of responding to stress are dangerous: they can lead to verbal and physical abuse, divorce, disease, and death. You will learn how you can vanquish the dragon's ways and replace them with the 8 steps.

The word *vanquish* beautifully depicts our goal. The Merriam Webster Dictionary gives two definitions. The first is "to overcome in battle or in a contest." The second is "to gain mastery over (as an emotion)." This is precisely our goal: gaining mastery over the anxiety, fear, anger, and depression that arise in our daily encounter with the dragon of dependency and desire.

I

Mastering Four Inner Steps for Stress

Week One

The Physical Step

Entering the Dragon's Cave of Transformation

THE WORDS SLAY THE DRAGON SEEM TOO VIOLENT for some people. But the archetypal imagery describes an inner event that requires decisive action. Therapy often uses the aggressive description of *breaking* ineffective patterns. We need an immediate, penetrating intervention to *interrupt* the reptile brain's repetitive pattern of fight-or-flight. Over time, these patterns become entrenched in the chemistry and wiring of the brain.

Our characteristic ways of responding to stress become fixed in the chemistry and circuitry of the brain. Moreover, the electrical impulses pass along the neural nets in the brain so that we simply continue to respond to stressful situations as we always have. This might be with anxiety, anger, or depression. To find our freedom to create new, more effective responses, we need to snip and rewire the twisted wires in the brain. We need to create new channels. Whether we think in terms of wires or channels, we need to realize that it is within our power to recondition and replace old, ineffective stimulus-response patterns with more effective ones.

We can learn to hold our distress, anxiety, anger, and depression in the arms of our awareness, like a mother holds and soothes her crying baby. Our breath does that for us. At the same time that we need tenderness, we need an aggressive and decisive awareness. In effect, we need a deepening and softening awareness along with a penetrating, focused awareness. We ned to be embracing and penetrating. Soft and firm.

When I did my initial research on stress, I found simple awareness of tension helped people relax. Simple awareness led to reduced tension in the large skeletal muscles. However, the use of slow-deep-belly breaths, self-talk, and the imagery of warmth and heaviness helped reduce tension in the smooth muscles.

Stress causes the smooth muscles around the blood vessels to constrict and slow blood flow. The imagery of warmth and heaviness flowing down through you as you imagine sitting in a hot tub relaxes the smooth muscles and allows blood to flow freely.

"*That's How I Feel! I Can't Change How I Feel!*"

Once stress strikes, we must enter the dragon's cave. We do this by slow-deep-belly breathing. Entering the dragon's cave means making a space within which we can fully feel without acting on our dragon-driven desires, emotions, and actions.

In my clinical practice, I came up with a device to help people realize how they can change feelings. So often, people would say, "That's how I feel." It was as if feelings were written in stone. School-age children would say to their parents, "I don't feel like doing my homework."Feelings like these can be changed.

The letters I-D-E-A are a way to describe how mental images occur in a rapid-fire manner. Then a desire emerges along with an emotion leading to an action. A mental I-image of a sandwich pops into my mind. I feel hungry and a D-desire to eat emerges and and an E-emotion (my love of that particular food) impels me to the A-action of making or ordering the desired food.

In order to change and counter a pattern, we can rearrange the letters I-D-E-A into A-I-D-E. These four letters can *aid* us in establishing new feelings and habit patterns. A reluctant student can just sit down and begin to do homework. The A-action can conjure up a motivating I-image of getting a good grade. This can create a channel within which the D-desire and E-emotion can flow so that the student is now motivated to keep studying.

The same holds true for slaying the strong motivation of the dragon and the emergency reflex it activates. We simply take action contrary to the emergency reflex, namely, the innate quieting reflex. This is the reflex that restores us to balance and homeostasis once the perceived threat, the stress, has passed.

We activate the quieting reflex by taking specific actions: relaxing our abdominal muscles and taking slow-deep-belly breaths to counter the rapid-shallow-chest breaths of the emergency reflex; smiling inwardly by twinkling our eyes, and slightly raising the corners of our mouth to counter the mask of tension and fixed stare of the emergency reflex; and finally, silently saying c-o-o-l as we inhale, and c-a-l-m as we exhale. This helps us feel cool and calm so that we can be more effective in the face of personal and interpersonal stress and conflict. The actions lead to an image of being cool and calm, and we experience the desire and emotions to continue feeling cool and calm.

Recognizing: Practicing the First Skill of the Physical Step

• Practice recognizing as quickly as possible when you're hooked by a stressful situation. Simply practice identifying the physical sensations that tell you that you are feeling tense.

• What do you tend to notice first when stress strikes? Perhaps you notice the typical negative emotions that can occur when stress strikes: anger, anxiety, or depression. Or you may notice that you are feeling the offshoots of anger, anxiety, and depression such as bitterness, resentment, hostility, nervousness, or disappointment. Then again, maybe you first notice your actions such as you are yelling or raising your voice or being critical and fault-finding.

• Do you tend to be more aware of the situation first? Do you notice that you are stuck in traffic before you notice how tense and angry you are? Do you notice someone is yelling at you and criticizing you before you notice that you are scared and anxious or angry and hurt? The key is to notice that you are stressed.

Resisting: Practicing the Second Skill of the Physical Step

• Each time you notice you are stressed, whether by identifying a physical, emotional, or situational aspect of stress, picture a big red stop sign. Silently shout in your head: "STOP!" Then immediately take a slow-deep-belly breath. You *stop* yourself from acting or speaking. You say and do nothing. Instead, you begin to take slow-deep-belly breaths. This kind of breathing is how you slay the dragon's physical aspect: the illusion generated by the reptile brain that your only option is fight-or-flight.

• Slaying the dragon means cutting the cord of our dependency on someone or something external to ourselves to find relief from stress. We must cut the cord of our residual, reactive dependency. For the prolonged physical dependency of childhood leads us to act as if we are dependent on something external to ourselves to feel good and be at peace. This belief is based on the fact that we come into the world completely helpless.

• Our first stress is relieved in our mother's arms. Now, instead of our mother's arms or soothing words, we turn to our own breath and the arms of our own awareness. We no longer need to control others as we sever the cord and set ourselves free. We can calm and soothe ourselves with our own awareness, self-talk, and breath.

• As you breathe in, remind yourself that your feeling good and being at peace DO NOT depend on something out there, but do depend on you taking charge and taking a breath. Just keep practicing the formula of *recognizing* you are stressed, *resisting* the impulse to say or do anything except silently shouting, "STOP!"

• As you breathe slowly and deeply, silently say to yourself, "Breathing in, I stop and still my mind. Breathing out, I stop and still my body." Next, breathe in and silently say, "I can keep my mind c-o-o-l." And, breathing out, silently say, "my body c-a-l-m no matter what." Next, just keep silently repeating "c-o-o-l mind" as you breathe in, and "c-a-l-m body" as you breathe out. Then just silently repeat "c-o-o-l" as you slowly inhale.

• Finally, just practice silently saying c-o-o-l as you breathe in. Now as you breathe out, silently say c-a-l-m. Draw out c-o-o-l and c-a-l-m while you focus on *enjoying* the pleasurable sensations of a cool head and a calm body.

Relaxing: Practicing the Third Skill of the Physical Step

• Reciprocal inhibition is a physiological principle that indicates that one brain state inhibits another. In short, we can't be tense and relaxed at the same time. We can't be anxious and relaxed. Nor can we be assertive and anxious. We *resist* reacting, and then we relax.

• A simple slow-deep-belly breath slays the dragon. You can prove this to yourself. Take a deep breath. Be sure to breathe into your belly, not your chest. Belly breathing is more deeply relaxing. Breathing into the chest keeps the stress response activated. Notice how good it feels to take a slow-deep-belly breath. "

• Imagine you're in a situation you wish you could escape from such as being stuck in traffic, sitting in a boring class or meeting, or being reprimanded by a boss who reminds you of your over-bearing father. Do some slow-deep-belly breathing. Remind yourself of how the physical act of breathing can begin to help you feel good and be at peace. Silently say to yourself, "Breathing in cool, I AM NOT dependent on escaping from here right now to feel good and be at peace. Breathing out calm, I remind myself that I can feel good in the moment by doing slow-deep-belly breathing.

• Practice taking some slow-deep-belly breaths. With each breath, let your jaw, tongue, and shoulders go limp as you exhale. And feel a wave of warmth and heaviness flow down through your body and out the soles of your feet. To facilitate relaxing your jaw, gently clench your teeth. Then, when you exhale, let your jaw drop even as you keep your mouth closed. You'll feel your top and bottom rows of teeth separate. Imagine you are in a hot tub up to your neck in comfortably hot, swirling water. Your head feels cool since the hot tub is outside on a deck. It is a cool, crisp night, and you see the stars shining. Your body is warm and relaxed while your head is cool and clear. Use this visual of the hot tub set in the cool night air in order to help you achieve a cool, alert mind, and a relaxed body. An alert mind and relaxed body help make you most effective in the face of stress and conflict.

• Practice feeling good. Throughout your day do the following: Breathe in and silently say, "Breathing slowly and deeply like this feels so good." Now exhale and silently say, "And breathing out slowly like this also makes me feel so good."

• Each time you identify that you are stressed, stop and breathe. Practice breathing slowly and deeply by relaxing your abdominal muscles. You then do belly breathing. Remember, instead of sucking in your stomach as you breathe in, relax and let your belly expand. As you breathe out, let you belly contract. Belly rises as you inhale. And belly falls as you exhale. Next, in order to make sure you are breathing slowly, breathe in, silently saying one . . . two . . . . three . . . four . . . five. Then exhale slowly silently counting backwards: five . . . four . . . three . . . two . . . one. By stopping and breathing, we engage our higher brain functions so we can calm ourselves. We do this by relaxing with the breath, and by using self-talk to produce a cool mind and a calm body.

Breathing Affirmations Defeat the Dragon's Addictive Ways

Addictions involve instantly reacting to an impulse. We want to yell, criticize or complain. We find ourselves reaching for a cigarette, beer, another glass of wine, or a piece of chocolate cake. We need to experience *both* the itch and the urge to scratch. That is, to conquer our addictions, we need to experience the discomfort *and* the urge to do something to remove that discomfort.

• Picture a big red stop sign, and yell in your head, not out loud, "STOP!" Resist the impulse. Then relax by breathing and watching the impulse to yell, reach for comfort food, or to smoke a cigarette, or reach for alcohol. Remember, we reach for something, or do something to help us feel good and to stop feeling bad. (Note: Silently say the following and do slow-deep-belly breathing.)

• Breathing in cool, I DO NOT need_____(a cigarette, a piece of cake, a drink of alcohol, etc.) to feel good and be at peace. Breathing out calm, I can feel good and be at peace by enjoying a series of slow-deep-belly breaths."

• Now tell yourself, "My desiring to reach for_____(a cigarette, a piece of cake, a drink, etc.) is telling me that I hate this discomfort. And that's because I'd love to feel relieved and calm."

* * *

The primary focus of this week is to prove to yourself that you *can* feel good by stopping and taking slow-deep-belly breaths when stress strikes. The goal of the week is to realize you DO NOT have to resort to the dragon's reactive ways of trying to feel good: aggression (fight) or repression and depression (flight).

This week you practice approaching stress with a relaxed body and an alert mind. By simply being aware that you are stressed, you begin to relax your large muscles. And then you relax even more deeply by doing the slow-deep-belly breathing coupled with self-talk and the imagery of warmth and heaviness flowing through you as you imagine yourself in a hot tub from the neck down. Now start practicing S-stopping and breathing when you feel stressed.

Week Two

The Mental Step

SHIFT YOUR FOCUS & YOUR ENERGY FOLLOWS

I DEFINE STRESS AS THE *PRESSURE* WE FEEL FROM THE PERCEIVED GAP between what we would love to have happen and our ability to attain what we would love. The dragon in us responds to this gap with anxiety and fear, anger and rage, sadness and depression.

The mental step enables us to shift our focus from fear and anger to a focus on what we would love to have happen. Before we go into how we make this shift with the mental step, we will explore the power that our focus wields over our emotions and energy.

We slay the dragon mentally by initiating the inner quest. The dragon focuses on the outer quest. And so when we initiate the inner quest, we slay the dragon's focus on the external world. As I have said in *Love Conquers Stress*, the word question has the word *quest* in it. So one way to initiate the inner quest is with a question.

With the mental step, we use an implied question by employing a sentence-completion approach. Before we go into that, we can use a direct question based on the ABC approach to managing our emotions, originally developed by psychologist Albert Ellis. Once we realize we are feeling stressed, we can ask ourselves, "What am I telling myself about the situation I am finding stressful to *make* myself feel what I am feeling? What am I telling myself to make myself anxious, angry, or depressed?"

The ABC's of Stress Relief

When we are stressed there is an A-activating event (stressful situation) such as my boss is upset with my work performance. Immediately, there is a C-consequence. In this case I might be anxious or angry. But why am I anxious or angry? The answer lies at B-beliefs, or I like to think of B as standing for brain. Our brain does a rapid-fire evaluation of what is going on in the external world. The boss is upset, and I am instantly anxious or angry. I could alternate between both. How is that possible? It depends on what I am T-telling myself, that is, what I B-believe, my beliefs in my brain, about the activating event.

The dragon in us drives us to try to control or run from the activating event. When the activating event is a loved one feeling upset, the attempt to control his or her distress can lead to conflict. In order to gain some control of our reptile-brain reaction, we STOP and ask ourselves, "What am I, in effect, rapidly telling myself?"

If you are anxious, you need to ask yourself, "What am I telling myself that makes me anxious?" You might be telling yourself, "I'm going to lose my job, and that would be disastrous! I don't know if I can find another job! My wife and kids depend on me!" If you are angry, you might be telling yourself, "My boss is being unfair. If he tries to fire me, I'll fight him on this. I'll call my union representative. He'll be sorry if he messes with me."

With the mental step, you do not use a direct question to initiate the inner quest. You slay the dragon with the sharp-focused awareness that is your sword of love. You slay the dragon's fear focus with a love focus. The love focus involves focusing on what you would love to have happen; whereas the fear focus zeroes in on what you are *afraid* will happen.

Our fear sends us into fleeing or getting angry and fighting. We become the dragon rearing up ready to fight, the flames of fear and anger shooting from our mouth. Or, we hide in the dark depths of our cave. Before we go into how we shift our focus, we need to explore the nature of our emotions.

Understanding Emotions as Focus & Energy

What are emotions? Do they have a cognitive component? Most definitely. Emotions tell us someone or something is important to us; and it is the energy of emotion that sets us in motion. The key to understanding and practicing the mental step is found in the first law of thermodynamics.

Energy can neither be created nor destroyed only changed.

The letter E in emotion can help us remember that emotions are E-ENERGY that sets us into MOTION. Love is the primary emotion from which all other emotions emerge. The energy of love moves us to take care of and cherish the people, places, and things we love. If we didn't care we wouldn't feel mad, sad, or glad.

For the sake of simplicity, we can separate our basic negative emotions into three sets: anger and rage, fear and anxiety, sadness and depression.

Our anger and rage tell us someone or something we love is in danger and move us to fight.

Our fear and anxiety tell us that someone or something we love and value is in danger and move us to flight.

Our sadness and depression tell us that someone or something we love and value is in danger of being lost or has been lost and move us to tears and acceptance of the loss.

If someone or something is in danger of being lost, we feel sad or depressed when we *believe* there is nothing we can do about preventing the loss. For a more detailed look at our negative emotions and their relationship to love, see chapter three in *8 Steps to Love*.

The Power of a Love Focus & Prisoner of War Survivors

With the mental step, we further penetrate and uproot the implied belief that we are dependent on something external to ourselves to feel good and be at peace. The stories of prisoner of war survivors

(POWS) who triumphed over their circumstances show us how we can unmask the drama of a fear focus and replace it with a love focus. It is as if the POWS said to themselves, "Breathing in cool, I AM NOT dependent on escaping from here right now to feel good and be at peace. Breathing out calm, I remind myself that I can feel good in the moment by breathing deeply and slowly." It is as if the POWS were telling themselves, "Breathing in cool, I DO NOT have to be depressed right now because I'm away from the people I love. Breathing out calm, I AM FREE to focus on remembering the people I love."

The POWS who committed suicide probably focused on the hopelessness and bleakness of being imprisoned. They probably maintained a fear focus, thinking, "I'll never get out of here."

The world renowned psychiatrist Victor Frankl not only survived imprisonment in a Nazi concentration camp, he shared important insights about it. He proclaimed, "You can take everything from a man but the last of the human freedoms, the freedom to choose your attitude in any given set of circumstances."

Frankl based his claim upon those individuals who went against the biological drive to survive. Though starving, these people would give others their last piece of bread. They chose to slay the dragon of dependency in themselves by focusing on love and compassion for others. Frankl himself found comfort in focusing his thoughts on his beloved wife. Frankl's observations reveal the power that a love focus has over a fear focus in one of the most horrible experiences people have had to endure.

Practicing the Mental Step: From a Fear Focus to a Love Focus

The key to this step is training yourself to *express* and not *repress* or *aggress* your stress. The dragon in us drives us to breathe fire at others (aggress) or to hide in our cave (repress) our stress.

• When stress strikes, you are to start with the symptom: sensation, feeling, fantasy image, and/or desire. For example, you begin with the pain in my chest, or my clenched jaw, or my fantasy of running away, or my image of seeing myself screaming. Then you add to the symptom the phrase that helps you shift your focus and energy. For example, "My fantasy of running away is telling me that I hate it that you are yelling at me. And that's because I'd love it if you would speak softly and respectfully to me." This is the crux of the mental step, and that's why I also call this step the shift your focus and energy technique. As you will see, the 8 steps condense into three core techniques. This is the first of the three.

The HEART of this Technique & Why We Use the Word Hate

The heart of this first technique is found in the letters of the word HEART. We take the step to HEAR with our heart what our anger, anxiety, or depression is T-telling us so that we can T-transform the dragon's fear focus into a love focus. And later on, in the four outer steps, we will be learning to HEAR with our heart what our loved ones' anger, anxiety, or depression is T-telling them so that they can T-transform their fear focus into a love focus.

• We will add the brief versions of the emotional and spiritual steps. That means you will shift your focus and energy from what you hate to what you love. And then you O-observe the stress gap between what you would love to have happen and your ability to attain what you would love. You continue your inner quest with the question, "Is there anything I can do to coolly and calmly close the gap?" Depending on your answer, you then go to the spiritual step. You P-proceed to do whatever you can, or turn to prayer and ask for help from your higher power as defined by your personal beliefs.

• We use the word hate because it can fill us with the power and energy of passion. We *harness hate* as a springboard toward attaining what we would love. The other reason, which we'll go into with the emotional step, is to weaken our mental and emotional defenses. Eventually, we don't need to use hate. We can skip right to love.

• There is a tendency in relaxation training to tense each set of muscles we want to relax before we relax them. This helps us feel the *contrast* which fosters relaxation. For practice, as you say the phrase: "My anger, anxiety, or depression is telling me that I hate it that or when_____." Squat down. Make two fists in front of your chest, and tense your body so that you can fully feel and express the contracted energy of your negative emotions. Then express, "And that's because I'd love it if_____." As you do, begin to stand up straight. Open your hands, and reach up as if to the heavens above. Notice how saying the word love *lifts* and *expands* your mood and energy.

Some Examples to Guide You in Practicing the Mental Step

Below are some examples you can use to guide you in practicing the mental step. The examples apply the mental step in the context of the four inner steps: S-stop, T-tell, O-observe, and P-proceed.

Transforming Panic Over a Missing Child

Sylvia is in a large department store with her three-year-old son Mason, and her ten-year-old daughter Melanie. Suddenly, Sylvia discovers that Mason is missing. She starts screaming his name. The store staff rush over to see what's wrong, and they call the store manager. All the doors are locked for just this kind of emergency. In five minutes, Mason is found hiding. He was playing hide-and-seek. Rather than yell at him and scold him, Sylvia hugs him. Through her tears, she tells him, "You scared Mommy." Mason cries at seeing his mommy's tears.

Sylvia reviewed the stressful situation with me, and I helped her imagine applying the four steps. She first recalls feeling seized with fear and panic. She recalls her heart pounding as she gasps for her breath. She also recalls her mind being filled with the pictures of lost and abducted children on milk cartons and postcards the United States Postal Service sends out. She then remembers thinking, *Mason may be abducted, and I may never see him again!*

She now imagines silently shouting, "STOP!" Then she begins to breathe slowly and deeply into her belly while thinking, "Breathing in c-o-o-l, I stop and still my mind. Breathing out c-a-l-m, I stop and still my body." Then breathing in she thinks, "I can keep my mind c-o-o-l, and . . ." she pauses and exhales slowly, silently saying, "my body c-a-l-m no matter what."

Sylvia continues to think c-o-o-l as she breathes in and c-a-l-m as she breathes out. She then does the mental step where she T-tells herself, "My panic is telling me that I hate it that I do not see my son anywhere. And that's because I'd love to find him right now!"

Replacing her fear focus with a love focus, she O-observes the gap between what is—Mason is missing—and what she'd love—finding Mason. She continues her inner quest by asking herself, "What can I do to close the gap?" She answers, "I can notify the store staff and get them to help me look for Mason." Then she P-proceeds to contact staff for their help. In addition, she P-prays to God, as defined by her personal belief in Judaism, "Please help us find Mason."

Transforming Anger & Impatience While Standing in Line

Robert, a divorced man in his thirties, is standing in line at the grocery store. It is almost three o'clock, and he is supposed to pick up his ten-year-old son at school. Robert thought he'd make a quick stop at the store to pick up a few things for dinner that night. There are three people ahead of him. The one holding up the line is an elderly woman having a hard time hearing and following the instructions on using her debit card.

The store clerk is being patient. Minutes pass. Robert looks at his watch. If this line doesn't start moving, he's going to be late to pick up his son. It is Robert's day to pick up his son for visitation. One woman in front of him just leaves the grocery items she was going to buy on the conveyor belt, and leaves in a huff, cursing under her breath.

Robert is feeling his shoulders tense up. A fantasy of throwing his items down and leaving flashes through his mind. He is angry.

Robert reviewed with me the stressful situation, and I had him go through the steps. First, he imagines silently shouting, "STOP!" Then he does some slow-deep-belly breathing. He pairs c-o-o-l with his inhales and c-a-l-m with his exhales.

Then he T-tells himself, "My feeling like throwing my stuff down and leaving is telling me that I hate it that this old woman is taking so long. And that's because I'd love it if she'd hurry up! My anger is telling me I hate it that the clerk is letting her hold up this line. And that's because I'd love it if the clerk would call the store manager over. The manager could take the woman aside and finish her transaction at the customer service counter."

Armed with a love focus and not a fear focus, Robert O-observes and fully faces the truth of the gap between what he would love and his ability to attain it. He continues the inner quest started with the mental step by asking, "What, if anything, can I do to close the gap?"

Robert decides there is nothing to do but just wait. He now takes the spiritual step, and P-proceeds to wait while doing his belly breathing. He pairs his inhales with a silent c-o-o-l and his exhales with a silent c-a-l-m. He also employs the gap-closing tool I call the mantra of compassion. (Mantra is from Sanskrit, and it means mental device.) He imagines looking at the elderly woman, and he silently says to her from his heart: "I know in my heart you would go faster if you could go faster, but you can't (not yet, anyway) so you don't." He may run late, but he also accepts the fact that he *chose* to fit this shopping in before picking up his son. Fully facing the truth of the sitess gap, he feels better.

Transforming Feeling Angry & Depressed at Home

Nancy, a thirty-year-old mother, just finished cleaning the floor, and she hears the squeaking sound of her teenage son's sneakers. She starts to picture black skid marks on the kitchen tile. She is ready to scream. Her face is flushed. All this is taking place in microseconds.

In reviewing the situation, Nancy does the steps of S-T-O-P. First she takes a breath while thinking, "Breathing in, I stop and still my mind, and breathing out I stop and still my body."

Breathing in, she thinks, "I can keep my mind cool," and breathing out, she thinks, "and my body calm no matter what!" She feels angry and depressed. She proceeds to T-tell herself, "My anger and depressed feelings are telling me I hate it that no sooner do I finish cleaning and my son messes up what I do. And that's because I'd love it if the house could stay clean for a week! Not just an hour!"

She then O-observes, and faces the truth of the gap between what she would love and what is. She continues the inner quest and asks, "What, if anything, can I do to close the gap?"

Nancy then P-proceeds to close the gap by thinking that she could make her son clean up his messes. But in the case of the kitchen floor, she realizes her son wouldn't do as good a job as she would. She concludes that she just has to accept that her cleaning is an ongoing job; it is just part of the package of being a stay-at-home mom. She feels good that she did *not* scream at her son.

Athletic Analogies for Replacing a Fear Focus with a Love Focus

• A basketball player is about to shoot a foul shot. The fans are screaming. He feels anxious. What can he do? He can bounce the ball a few times and tell himself, "My feeling anxious is telling me that I would hate to miss this shot." He gives expression to his fear leaving a vacuum for him to fill.

Then, as he begins the movement of shooting, he silently says, "And that's because I'd love to . . ." He visualizes the ball successfully going into the basket. By letting the word love *linger* on his lips and tongue, he fully focuses on the desired outcome, and he achieves it. He lets the "L" word *lift* him to achieving his goal. Silently saying *love* and letting the word linger on his lips until the releases the ball, keeps fear from flying back into his mind.

A golfer is facing a water hole, and if he hits around it, he will, at best, make par. If he hits over it, he could get on the green and go one or two under par. He decides to hit the ball over the water hole. What can he do? He can start his backswing thinking, "I would hate to hit the ball in the water." And then on his downswing, he thinks, "And that's because, I'd love to. . . ." He visualizes hitting the ball right onto the green."

Practicing Mental Step Affirmations for Slaying the Dragon

Note: Silently say the following, and do slow-deep-belly breathing.

• "Breathing in cool, I remind myself that, like the POWS, I AM NOT dependent on what is going on around me to feel good and be at peace. Breathing out calm, I remind myself I can feel good and be at peace by focusing on whom or what I love."

• "Breathing in cool, I remind myself that, like the POWS, I DO NOT feel good and at peace by maintaining a fear focus. Breathing out calm, I remind myself that I feel good and at peace by shifting to a love focus."

• "Breathing in cool, I DO NOT need to impress others to feel good and be at peace. Breathing out calm, I can feel good and be at peace by being free of the need to impress others."

* * *

The primary goal of this week is to prove to yourself that you *can* feel better when stress strikes by replacing the dragon's fear focus with a love focus. You focus on what you'd love to have happen instead of what you fear might happen. Athletic analogies nicely illustrate the *effectiveness* of a love focus over a fear focus. The following can help you practice shifting your focus and energy.

Remember, you may want to skip using the word hate once you get the hang of connecting the negative emotion to love. Instead, you would say something like, "My fear, anger, or depression is simply telling me that I'd love_____." Fill in the blank with what you would love to have happen.

Week Three

The Emotional Step

LOOK THROUGH THE PRESENT TO HEAL HIDDEN HURTS OF THE PAST

WITH THE EMOTIONAL STEP, WE OBSERVE AND FULLY FACE the truth of the perceived stress gap. This is the gap between what is and what we would love to have happen. We also O-observe whether the stress is one that occurs often. Is it a repeated relationship stress, rooted in the hidden hurts of your personal emotional history? In order to heal these hidden hurts, you do the look through technique. Before we go into this crucial technique, we need to learn about the dragon's defenses that get erected by the hurt child within us.

The Dragon, Your Idealized Self & Your Psychological Survival

The emotional aspect of the dragon of dependency and desire involves our primary need for approval. Early in our childhood, we construct an idealized self as a good boy or good girl in order to secure the love and approval of our parents.

Just as our physical survival is the domain of the dragon as our reptile brain, so the idealized self is defended by the dragon in the form of our dependency on and desire for others to love and admire us. This desire becomes linked with our psychological survival.

The idealized self strives for *perfection* to prevent *rejection*, first by our parents and then by others. Taken to the extreme, parental rejection equals death. I have found young children who feel rejected often have fears of being sent out into the cold to starve.

26

Like Narcissus in Greek Mythology, the idealized self focuses on being perfect. We strive to live up to what I call i*nner dictates*. We are not always conscious of these beliefs, these musts. If asked, we are likely to say, "Nobody's perfect. Everybody makes mistakes. Nobody looks good all the time." And yet, unconsciously, we may cling tightly to our dictates. We say one thing but our behavior implies a different belief: "I must *always* be right. I must *never* be wrong. I must *never* make or admit making a mistake."

These inner dictates once guaranteed our psychological survival as a small child. A person may unconsciously spend his or her whole life organized so as to never be criticized, yelled at, made fun of, belittled, and/or punished. These goals are linked to loss of parental love; and the dragon in us knows parental love is linked to our very survival physically and psychologically.

Feeling stressed, we may argue and defend our cherished self-image. Our defensiveness can lead to conflict with others. We may get anxious and angry when our idealized self is threatened. "I'm right! You're wrong!" This is the meta-message of our arguing. What hooks you and puts you on the defensive? Being told you're wrong? Being criticized? Not being listened to? Not being heard? Having to repeat yourself? Directly or indirectly being told you're stupid?

When stress strikes, and we overreact, we are often *hooked* by a feeling of helplessness. We may fly into fear, anxiety, anger, or depression. Having stronger feelings than the stressful situation warrants is often a sign that an emotional wound of a hidden hurt of our childhood or adolescence has been ripped open.

In penetrating our mental and emotional defenses, we can uncover the hidden hurt holding us back from effectively handling the present stress. Once we uncover the hurt, we discover where and when we were cut off from a love focus and developed a fear focus.

If we do not confront our personal emotional history so that we can uncover and heal our hidden hurts, we are doomed to tragically repeat the drama of our childhood. History *does* repeat itself.

The key elements of the drama remain the same: only the players change. Sometimes the players are your children or your love partner. At other times, the players are the people you work with.

The drama and roles rarely vary. As the lead player, you may exercise one of two options when stress strikes: victim or victimizer. You may reenact the role of powerless-persecuted child. Or, you may play the role of powerful-persecuting parent.

The fortress of our idealized self walls off our heart and our ability to focus on what we would love to have happen. We are frozen in fear which we may cover up with anger. Therefore, if one of your emotional challenges involves anger, then consider how anger is often a *defense* against feeling hurt. It may be part of your cherished self as someone who is not vulnerable to being hurt and taken advantage of by others.

This idealized self of being invulnerable is constructed out of the brick and mortar of the hidden hurts of your past, especially your early childhood hurts. These hurts and the anger erected to protect against the fear of being hurt again can be healed and released with the look through technique.

Practicing the Look Through Technique

By doing the look through technique, we cut through the defenses of our idealized self. The Narcissus in us dives into the dark pool of memory, and we reconnect to our innermost heart, our true self.

We look through the present to open the door to the past and see what hidden hurt is holding us in a fear focus. Looking through releases and helps us heal the hurt. Our capacity to achieve a love focus is restored. And we are no longer paralyzed in current situations that resemble the earlier circumstances where we were hurt.

The following are some examples of individuals applying the look through technique. One of the most prevalent examples is the repeated relationship stress experienced in our intimate love relationships.

In the examples that follow, notice how the mental and the emotional steps work together to address repeated relationship stress. Just as you are expressing your stress with the mental step (the shift your focus and energy technique), you notice that the stress you are feeling is familiar. Shifting your focus and energy helps *weaken* your defenses. You then look through the present situation and uncover the earlier situation rendering you helpless and hopeless.

Releasing Repeated Relationship Stress with a Boss

Susan was angry at her boss. She felt unappreciated compared to others in the office, notably the men. Not feeling appreciated was a repeated relationship stress that haunted her in other relationships as well. First, Susan recalled the last time she felt especially angry at her boss. She imagined what she would say to him if she did *not* have to worry about losing her job. This was not a rehearsal for what she might say someday. First, she S-stopped and did some slow-deep-belly breaths. Then she began to T-tell herself, "My unexpressed anger at you [her boss] is telling me that I hate it that you don't appreciate my ability. And that's because I'd love it if you would see and appreciate my work. My anger is telling me that I hate that you don't see me. And that's because I'd love it if you would see me!"

Then Susan proceeded to O-observe how familiar her anger felt to her. While fully feeling her anger at her boss, she looked through her boss to see whom she might remember feeling this way with in her family when she was growing up. She saw her father. The age that came to her was eight years old. She was proud of being in a school play. She had so wanted her father to see her. But he didn't make it. He went to her older brother's basketball game. She imagined saying to her father some of the same words that she had said to her boss, "My anger is telling me that I hate that you don't see me. See my ability. And that's because I'd love it if you would see me and be proud of me."

Wiping the tears away, Susan imagined hugging her eight-year-old self into her heart. She then P-proceeded to close the gap between what she would love to have happen with her boss, and what actually existed. She imagined sitting in his office and coolly and calmly saying, "I don't believe you see all that I do, and all that I am capable of doing. I want to see what I can do to help you realize what I can do." She could now be an adult dealing with her boss and not the enraged eight-year-old who was angry and afraid of confronting her father over favoring her brother.

Releasing Repeated Relationship Stress with a Daughter

Sally was often frustrated with her teenage daughter Marie. One day she told me that she yelled at Marie, "I hate you! After all I do to make you happy, I hate how you are never happy!" Sally yelled this in response to Marie's upset over her best female friend moving away.

Despite her feeling justified in her anger, later that evening, Sally had some awareness that her reaction was inappropriate. Marie's upset over her friend moving was not something Sally could solve. Nor was it her fault. It was not something Sally did. Sally reviewed the stressful moment and prepared to look through it.

Sally did the physical step of S-stopping and breathing. Then she did the mental step by T-telling herself, "My saying I hate you for never being happy is telling me that I hate it when you are unhappy. And that's because I'd love it if you were happy all the time."

Moving to the emotional step, Sally O-observed how familiar the feeling of her anger was, While she was fully feeling the anger, Sally looked through her daughter to see the person in her family when she was growing up to whom she could say the same words she said to Marie. She saw her mother. Sally was seven. She yelled, "I hate you! After all I do to please you, I hate how you're never happy!"

Tears filled her eyes as she remembered how hopeless and helpless she felt in the face of her mother's chronic unhappiness. She was able to see that her daughter's unhappiness had unconsciously reminded her of her mother. Sally imagined hugging the hurt seven-year-old back into her heart. She thought of other ages when she felt the same helplessness. She hugged those younger selves back into her heart, and returned her focus to the present.

Sally could see that there was nothing she could do about Marie's friend moving away. But she could begin to close her stress gap by

P-proceeding to be comforting and consoling to Marie. Sally also apologized to her daughter. She explained to Marie why she had reacted as she did. Sally had identified and begun to heal a hidden hurt of her past.

Releasing Repeated Relationship Stress with a Spouse

Sam was waking up in the night with his heart pounding, and his palms sweaty. He was dreaming that he was back in Vietnam. He was in the underground tunnels filled with water. At one end, the Viet-Cong were hiding. Rats swam past his face, and he couldn't move or make a sound. I asked him, "Where do you feel trapped and unable to move in your present life?" He told me that he felt immobilized in his marriage. "Sometimes I imagine my wife wearing combat boots. I sometimes call her the sergeant," he said.

"What would you say to your wife if you could express your true feelings?" I asked. I then said, "This is not a rehearsal for what you might actually say. Just express your uncensored feelings."

Familiar with the four steps, Sam S-stopped and began belly breathing. Then he began to T-tell himself as he pictured his wife, "My feeling immobilized is telling me that I hate it that you are so controlling of my every move. And that's because I'd love it if you would trust me and my judgment."

Sam O-observed how familiar this immobilized feeling felt so he looked through his wife. He saw his mother. He was nine years old. What he had said to his wife fit for his mother. He pictured his mother and said, "I hate how you try to control my every move. And that's because I'd love it if you would trust me." The other kids in his neighborhood were allowed to ride their bikes the half mile to the shopping center. Sam's mother wouldn't let him.

Sam had struggled to get free of her overly controlling grip. Now he was waking up at thirty-eight years old to realize he was married to a woman as controlling as his mother. Sam recalled other ages with something to say. He hugged into his heart the nine-year-old and the other ages who suffered under his mother's iron-fisted rule.

Sam now P-proceeded to close the gap between what he'd love to have happen, having his wife trust him and his judgment, and her current controlling actions. He resolved to coolly and calmly confront his wife on this issue. He didn't have to cower in the tunnel, caught between the rats and the Viet-Cong. He had survived that, and he needed to remember how the man he was had survived such horrifying circumstances.

Armed with a new sense of self, Sam could now *feel* the truth; he was no longer a little boy without a father to back him up with an overbearing mother. Sam could now be there for himself, for the little boy in his heart.

Releasing Repeated Relationship Stress Disguised as Road Rage

Ever since he first learned to drive, Roger repeatedly found himself enraged when he was driving. He was now forty years old, and he would still get as enraged as he did as an adolescent when other drivers cut him off. His rage went way beyond appropriate adult anger. He reviewed the last time he felt angry over being cut off.

First he S-stopped and began to do some slow-deep-belly breathing. Then he began to T-tell himself, imagining he was addressing the driver who cut him off, "My anger is telling me that I hate you cutting me off. And that's because I'd love it if you were more considerate and respectful."

Knowing the drill, Roger then O-observed how familiar his anger was, and he looked through the present to the past. He looked to see to whom in his family, when he was growing up, he could say the same words, or similar words. He saw his father, and the first age he remembered feeling like this was when he was five.

Roger recalled trying to excitedly tell his father about his day, and his father cut him off. He began talking about his day. This was a pattern of his father that persisted until the present. Roger was forty years old and his father was seventy. The father had always been the peacock showing off his plumage, and Roger was cut off from expressing himself to his father. He imagined speaking to his father first as a five-year-old, then as a teenager, and finally as an adult. "I hate when you cut me off! And that's because I'd love it if you were interested in me and my feelings." Then he imagined hugging into his heart the hurt five-year-old, and the hurt adolescent he once was; both felt enraged over being cut off by his self-absorbed father.

Roger then returned his focus to the present and P-proceeded to close the gap by resolving to have a man-to-man talk with his father. He did. And for once, his father listened. When Roger finished, his father apologized. Nothing could correct the past. But Roger could begin to heal the hurt and stop displacing his rage onto drivers who cut him off. He would be angry for a moment but not enraged and ready to jump out of the car and kill someone.

Hugging the Hurt Child in the Arms of Your Awareness

• After you do the look through and confront the situation   where you were cut off from love, you can focus on your breath again. As you imagine hugging the hurt child in you back into your heart, you can cradle that child in the arms of your awareness by breathing slowly, and deeply. Think of your breath as a mother's arms cradling and comforting her distressed baby. You cradle and comfort the child you with your slow-deep-belly breathing.

See the child you now relieved and happy. Now you imagine inhaling the smiling child into the arms of your heart. As you exhale, imagine that you are *blowing away* the child's hurt. Inhale love and comfort for the child you, and exhale the pain that child endured. You are now capable of a love focus where you were once hooked on a fear focus.

• Are there any other ages (younger selves) who need to express this issue? Have each of the other ages do so. You have drained the pain of the past hurt. Imagine lovingly hugging your younger selves into your heart. This is how you learn to love yourself. Now come back to the present and state with a firm resolve what you'd love the present person (love partner, friend, boss, colleague, etcetera) to do.

• If you are doing this with your love partner, repeat with other stresses. Take turns. Commit to helping each other drain past pain.

Practicing Emotional Step Affirmations for Slaying the Dragon

Note: Silently say the following and do slow-deep-belly breathing.

• "Breathing in cool, I do not need to blame others for *making* me feel and act in a certain way to feel good and at peace. Breathing out calm, I can feel good and be at peace by being emotionally independent and taking full responsibility for how I feel and act."

• "Breathing in cool, I don't need to put others down to feel good. Breathing out calm, I can feel good and be at peace by treating others with acceptance, compassion, and empathy."

• "Breathing in cool, I remind myself that I DO NOT need you to agree with me to feel good and be at peace. Breathing out calm, I remind myself that I can calmly listen to your disagreements and still feel good and be at peace."

* * *

The focus for this week is on practicing the look through technique. Remember that your true self harbors your real feelings. You deny these feelings, and you are cut off from the love in the core of your being and the ability to achieve a love focus over a fear focus.

With the shift your focus and energy and look through techniques, you shatter the illusion fostered by the the dragon. Your negative emotions are *not* separate from love. You know that love is the emotion that fuels all others. And remember, you wouldn't be mad, sad, or glad unless you loved and cared.

To reconnect with your true self, with the love you are at the core of our being, you must cut through your defenses. You must be the dragon-slaying hero in order to set free your true self symbolized by the treasure and/or princess guarded by the dragon.

Week Four

The Spiritual Step

ASK & FOLLOW THE SYNCHRONICITY (SIGNS)

A MAN DRIVING HOME FROM THE DENTIST SUDDENLY decides to stop and get a loaf of sourdough bread. He likes sourdough bread but isn't really craving it. It turns out his wife is home sick, and he doesn't know it. After he gets the bread, he has the thought, *I have to stay away from her. She's sick.* He is not sure who the she is he is thinking about. Mother? Sister? Wife?

He calls his wife to tell her he picked up a loaf of sourdough bread. She says, "Oh, you got my message." She had left a message on his cell phone asking him to pick up sourdough bread to go with soup. In her message, she also tells him that she felt sick after he left for work, and she decided to stay home. He got the message but not by checking his cell-phone messages.

What does this little incident show us? We are not separate; we are connected, especially to those we love. We are not just our body, and we can communicate without the restrictions and limitations of the body.

The essence of the spiritual step is to P-proceed to close the stress gap with the expansive energy and peaceful power of love. In my training and during my practice, I have met people who told me about their near-death experiences. When I was in graduate school, I met Dr. Raymond Moody who did the first research on the near-death experience. A few years after that, I heard Dr. Kenneth Ring speak about his research on near-death experiences.

He spoke to the psychology department when I was on my internship. From talking with these two researchers and to friends and patients of mine who had near-death experiences, I was struck by two things. People reporting near-death experiences are clinically dead for minutes and are not brain damaged. And, as Raymond Moody pointed out, these people get information during the near-death experience without the use of their body lying lifeless on the operating table. Kenneth Ring reported cases of congenitally blind people seeing perfectly during their near-death experience.

Kenneth Ring also reported the case of a woman who had a heart attack. After she was resuscitated, she reported how she had floated out of her body lying in the coronary care unit of the hospital. During her out-of-body experience, she noticed a tennis shoe on the ledge of the north wing of the hospital. She described it in detail, including the fact that one of the laces of the shoe was tucked under its heel. A hospital social worker investigated the woman's claim. She found the shoe: everything about the shoe was accurate right down to the lace tucked under the heel.

Near-death experiences suggest that our essence is spiritual, not physical. Ring reported that the personality changes following near-death experiences were lasting. People tended to put being a more loving and kind person as their top priority. The appearance of a loving being of light and deceased loved ones after one dies, suggest that the core of who we are is the peaceful power of love, and we are connected to a higher power of love.

As Saint John expressed it: "God is love; and he that dwelleth in love, dwelleth in God, and God in him" (1 John 4:16). As you practice the spiritual step, you can think of how the core of you is love, and, inasmuch as God is love, then you have the ultimate power in the universe residing within your heart.

Practicing Closing the Stress Gap with the Spiritual Step

Spiritus, the Latin word for spirit, literally means *breath.* Breath is the life-giving force. Connecting the breath with our spirit is part of the ancient spiritual notion of the invisible world of spirit, the spiritual realm, supporting the visible world of matter. Think of taking a slow-deep-belly breath as a way of connecting with your higher spiritual power, God, as defined by your personal beliefs.

Closing the Gap with the Breath

• Breathe in slowly and deeply, and silently say, "The inner peace of my spirit . . ." pause, and as you exhale, silently say, "is just a breath away." Repeat this at different times during the day. Just notice that you are feeling stressed. Shout, "STOP!" Then remind yourself the peace of your spirit is just a breath away by breathing and saying the words above. Remember, the connection with your *spirit* and *breath* has been around a long time: it was recognized by the ancients.

Closing the Gap with the Mantra of Compassion

One day as I was reflecting on the word peace, I had the thought that P-peacE-equals A-acceptance, C-compassion, and E-empathy. We can apply this acronym to dealing with others when we are upset with them. When dealing with a person we are upset with, we can proceed to close the gap by using what I have come to call the mantra of compassion.

We look at the person, or picture the person, and silently say, while breathing in, "I know in my heart that you would have done differently if you could have but you couldn't so you didn't." This mantra helps us find peace. We are simply adjusting our expectations to fit the perceived gap between what we would love to have happen with this troublesome person and what *is* happening.

It is important to note that the wording of the mantra is in past tense and not in present tense: *couldn't* and *didn't* are used instead of *can't* and *don't*. The actual truth is that the person's behavior is in the immediate past. If you want to use can't and don't to help you stop trying to make them understand your position, you can, but you want to keep open to the possibility that the person might be able to change their troublesome behavior someday.

So if you use can't instead of couldn't, you add after can't (not yet, anyway). This mantra helps us make peace with what is without struggling to change it. It is the essence of what is called Insight or Mindfulness Meditation. You'll be presented with a version of this kind of meditation in chapter ten.

Closing the Gap by Thanking Stress or Thanking Your Enemy

I'll never forget the wonderful experience I had during a very close college basketball game. We won by one point in the last ten seconds. The whole game was close: we were two well-matched teams. It just happened that I, as my team's leading scorer, was guarding and being guarded by the opposing team's leading scorer.

Right after the game began, the opposing team's leading scorer made a beautiful move on the baseline and scored a reverse lay-up. We were jogging right next to each other as my team was about to go on offense. With sincere admiration,, I said to him, "Great move!" He looked a little surprised to hear his opponent appreciating the shot he made. Still, he seemed to take it in and enjoy it.

Minutes later, when I got the ball, I made a move on him and scored. He followed my lead and gave me what appeared to be a sincere compliment. Throughout the game, we expressed appreciation when each other scored. I really did admire his lithe and graceful moves. By the end of the game, each of us led our teams by scoring over twenty points. Reflecting in the locker room after the game, I realized that, at some level, I loved and admired the excellence of my opponent. My enemy, my opponent, brought out the best in me, and I helped bring out his best as well. Suddenly, I could appreciate how we can follow the teaching of Jesus to love our enemies. Our enemies can help us be the best we can be.

The same is true for the enemy that any stress or conflict in life can be. Dr. Shelley Stockwell brought to my attention that the word tormentor has the word *mentor* in it. This can be used as a reminder that your tormentor is indeed your greatest mentor. By learning what stress hooks our heart, we can see what it is we need to work on so that we can become free.

Here is how you can thank the person or situation stressing you. Begin with a slow-deep-belly breath. Silently say to the person or situation. "Breathing in cool, thank you for reminding me of how I *don't* want to be a person who is_____. Breathing out calm, thank you for reminding me how I want to be a person who is_____." You can drop the phrase "a person who is" and just fill in the blanks with words that describe how you *don't* and *do* want to be.

For example, Albert, a married man in his forties, was complaining about how stressed he would get in reaction to his wife getting anxious and hysterical over stressful events in her life. I suggested Albert try *silently* saying the following to his wife when her being stressed started to stress him. "Breathing in cool, thank you for reminding me of how I don't want to be_____(anxious and hysterical when stress strikes). Breathing out calm, thank you for reminding me how I want to be_____(calm and peaceful when stress strikes)."

I told him that he could take it a step further, and say a prayer of gratitude, "Breathing in cool, thank You, (God) that I do not get anxious like my wife. Breathing out calm, thank You for the ability to stay calm, and please help me help her, or help her directly, develop this ability." This prayer helped Albert replace irritation with gratitude for his ability, and compassion and empathy for his wife.

Recall people and situations where you could thank the stress for reminding you how you don't want to be as a person, and how you prefer to be. You could use the words hate and love to inject more passion into your position. For example, Bill, a twenty-seven-year-old grocery-store clerk, told me about his stress on the job. He would feel angry with people who would block the aisles in the store with no awareness of others. They would act as if they were the only person in the world. He saw this as rude and inconsiderate. He tried *thanking stress* before asking them to move aside.

He would stand for a few seconds and repeat silently, "Breathing in cool, thank you for reminding me of how I don't want to be rude, inconsiderate, and oblivious to others. Breathing out calm, thank you for reminding me of how I want to be considerate and aware of others."

Closing the Gap with Prayer & Synchronicity

Synchronicity is defined as a meaningful coincidence between an inner event (concern, worry, thought, feeling) and an outer event. For example, a young man told me how he had moved to Colorado from Connecticut. One day he was beginning to wonder if he had made a mistake. He prayed for a moment while he was driving along. "God, should I stay out here? Am I accomplishing anything or going nowhere?" He was abruptly shaken out of his reverie by a large truck that, in passing him, forced him to turn off the road onto a side street. He looked up at the street sign: it read Nowhere Lane. He knew in his heart he needed to return home.

Samantha, a thirty-year-old woman afraid of committing to marriage, prayed for insight into her pattern of breaking off engagements. That night, she turned on the TV to see if there were any movies coming on.

As soon as she turns on the set, Samantha sees Julia Roberts speaking to Richard Gere. She is saying, "Benedict. Eggs Benedict. I love Eggs Benedict. I hate all other kinds of eggs." Samantha recognizes the scene as one of the final scenes from the film *Runaway Bride.* Samantha remembers that earlier in the film, Ike, (Richard Gere) is a reporter who asks each of the men Maggie (Julia Roberts) left at the altar how she liked her eggs. They all said, "just like me." One said, "scrambled with dill;" another said, "fried;"and the next said, "poached."

Samantha recalls that in this scene, Maggie is apologizing to Ike. They fell in love and were to be married. Maggie ran from Ike just as she had from all the others. The difference was that she ran from the others because they didn't know her; she ran from Ike because he did. The problem, Samantha recalls, was that Maggie didn't know herself. The Eggs Benedict comment was suggesting she was now beginning to know herself, and she was ready for marriage.

Samantha sees the synchronicity. She realizes she is afraid of losing herself in a marriage as her mother had done. Like Maggie, Samantha is a runaway bride; she is afraid she will just accommodate her desires to those of her husband. She resolves to focus on getting to know herself: her likes and dislikes so she can hold her own in a relationship.

• Breathing in, silently ask yourself, "Is there anything else I can do to close the gap?" Pause, then, addressing your higher power, breathe out thinking, "If not, then I let go and let *You* take over."

• If you are still upset, then pray to your higher power. Breathing in silently say, "Please help me see this situation in a new light so I can," breathing out, "let go of my pain (anger, fear, depression), feel better, find peace and resolution."

• You can also use a variation of the serenity prayer. Breathing in, addressing your higher power, "Please help me accept what I can't change and change what I can." Then breathing out, say, "And please help me know the difference." The key is to relax, watch, and listen to what comes.

• You then need to HEAR and feel with your heart what the synchronicity is "T" telling you. If you are facing a conflict then proceed with the peaceful power of love to apply the four outer steps.

Pennies from Heaven: A Game for Tuning into Synchronicity

There's a little game I play with God, the Divine Beloved, my higher power. I call it pennies from heaven. The Mayan shamans taught me that God, the Divine, talks to us all the time through nature. However, God, the Divine, is not restricted to the natural world to give us messages. Turn on your radio and a song you hear speaks to something going on in your love life. Here's how pennies from heaven works. I look at the year printed on the pennies I receive for change when I buy something. Then I consider what was going on in my life in that year, and I consider if what happened in that year has a message for now. For example, just yesterday, I was checking out at the grocery store. My change included four pennies: `1993, 1998, 2005, and 2006. *Were there separate messages?* I wondered. *Or one central one?* Then I realized that there had been something on my mind about taking time to write another book before booking more speaking engagements.

There was the message. In 1993, I received my first messages that I needed to start writing despite my extremely busy private practice. In 1998, my first book was published. In 2005, I finished my fifth book, and I completed updated revisions for the other four books. And the book you are holding in your hands was scheduled for release in 2006. I felt I had received confirmation from the Divine that I was on the right path. As I looked at the shiny new penny, I realized that this was the first 2006 penny I had seen.

Sychronicity is not only with pennies but involves anything or anyone that happens to cross our path in the course of our daily life. I have come to call these meaningful moments the Daily Dialogue with the Divine

In my book *A Matter of Love,* I detail my experiences of this daily dialogue as it occurred during the writing of the book. For example, one Sunday night, I took a break from writing, and flipped on the TV. An episode of the detective show *Dragnet* was just starting.

Then, just minutes into the show, I hear detective Joe Friday say, "My mother used to say, 'Evil is an absence of empathy.'" He was surprised by the lack of feeling on the part of the sister of a murdered woman. The woman passed judgment on her dead sister; she felt her sister was evil and not a Christian like her.

When I stopped writing, I was about to start the chapter entitled *Unmasking Evil.* I had planned to open the chapter with the quotation: "Evil is a defense against suffering." The third section of *A Matter of Love* is called, *The Return: Empathy.* I felt the Divine was guiding me to put the emphasis on how people who commit evil acts have no empathy for others. I was stunned at the synchronicity.

Living your life in moment-to-moment communion with God, the Divine, is a goal of the great sacred traditions. I believe this communion can be achieved through prayer and watching the synchronicity you receive in response to your prayers.

The spiritual teachings of the great spiritual masters of East and West aim to help us realize our connection with the spirit of God within us. That's what these great spiritual masters did and what they strive to help us do.

Spiritually speaking, connecting with the spirit of God within you is your greatest ally in mastering the stress and conflict of life. And that spirit is love. Making this connection to love is the goal of the spiritual step.

Practicing Spiritual Step Affirmations for Slaying the Dragon

Note: Silently say the following and do slow-deep-belly breathing.

•"Breathing in cool, I remind myself that I AM NOT dependent on my possessions to feel good and be at peace. Breathing out calm, I feel good and at peace by realizing I AM dependent on You, God, the ultimate power in the universe, to feel good and be at peace."

• "Breathing in cool, I remind myself that I DO NOT need to prove to you that I am right and you are wrong to feel good and be at peace. Breathing out calm, I remind myself that I can feel good and be at peace by breathing in slowly and deeply."

• "Breathing in cool, I AM NOT dependent on being loved to feel good and be at peace. Breathing out calm, I can feel good and be at peace by loving myself and others."
• "Breathing in cool, I remind myself that I AM NOT dependent on anything external to myself to feel good and be at peace. Breathing out calm, I remind myself that I have everything within

my heart—where love, the ultimate power in the universe, resides—to feel good and be at peace."

• "Breathing in cool, I remind myself that I AM NOT dependent on your approval to feel good and be at peace. Breathing out calm, I remind myself that I need my own approval to feel good and be at peace."

• "Breathing in cool, I remind myself that I AM NOT dependent on you liking me to feel good and be at peace. Breathing out calm, I remind myself that as long as I like myself I can feel good and be at peace."

• "Breathing in cool, I remind myself that I AM NOT dependent on living up to your standards to feel good and be at peace. Breathing out calm, I remind myself that I have only to live up to my own standards to feel good and be at peace."

"Breathing in cool, I remind myself that I don't need you to change for me to feel good and be at peace. Breathing out calm, I remind myself that I can feel good and be at peace by simply loving and accepting you as you are."

* * *

The focus for this week is on practicing paying attention to the synchronicity that occurs in your daily life. When you pray, pay particular attention to what happens after you finish. Focus on all that happens, and consider all that happens as related to your request. Even if what occurs does not seem related, consider the possibility of relating what happens to whatever stress or concern you are facing in your current life. Refer to the examples in this chapter to help you get the hang of the daily dialogue with the Divine.

II

Mastering Four Outer Steps for Conflict

Week Five

Listen, Open, Validate & Express

LEARNING TO LISTEN BEFORE YOU EXPRESS YOUR FEELINGS

"My husband doesn't listen to me." . . . "My wife doesn't understand.". . . "My parents don't understand." Not feeling listened to, heard, and understood were the common complaints I heard from people consulting me. I saw how not feeling heard was at the root of many conflicts. At the same time, I saw how the dragon of our dependency and desire was at work as well when people were faced with the stress of their loved ones being upset.

Whatever the content of the conflict, two meta-messages came up often. The first one was, "I NEED you to HEAR me!" And the second one was, "I NEED you to feel good, be at peace, and be happy *before* I can feel good, be at peace, and be happy."

We slay the dragon by listening instead of rescuing and solving. The hero in us needs to turn his or her attention away from the other person and stop the dragon in its tracks. Be patient. Help clarify the problem instead of rushing in and trying to solve it.

In almost all life circumstances, we determine what the problem is first before trying to fix it. I used to tell men, "You wouldn't lift up the hood of the car and start using your tools before determining what was wrong!" When dealing with other people's stress and upset, we are driven by the dragon of our dependency and desire.

The dragon drives us to eliminate the pain of others, especially the pain of our loved ones, as quickly as possible. The hero who rushes in to rescue is really riding the dragon, and not slaying it.

Men are not the only ones who do this; women are often guilty of trying to fix and reform their husbands. I came to see how, in many instances, conflicts are fueled by the best of intentions: the desire to relieve pain.

Origin of the Left Hand ((L-O-V-) / Right Hand (E) Technique

Jane, a woman in her forties, had just gone through a difficult divorce. She was seeing me for the stress and anxiety she was experiencing over the divorce, and over her teenage son. Her husband had been a bully. His hot temper and abusive actions were further ignited by alcohol.

Each week, Jane would come to see me panicky and frightened over being victimized by her sixteen-year-old son. He had stepped into the father's place by threatening and intimidating Jane. His actions went way beyond adolescent rebellion against parental authority.

On one occasion, she described how he had pinned her up against the wall. And, with his hostile, contorted face just inches from hers, he shouted vile epithets at her. He wasn't going to be responsive to her reasonable requests in any way, shape or form. He would do as he damn well pleased: he was the boss now that Dad was gone.

Sitting in session listening to Jane, I feared for her safety. Instead of taking time to listen to all her complaints, I felt compelled to get her started on assertiveness training so that she could stand up for herself, and, if need be, call the police. I would cut short the litany of complaints in order to help her review the scary situations and role play other options. When I bypassed her feelings, the assertiveness training and role playing didn't help her.

Then I realized that I was allowing *my* anxiety to get in the way. I was letting the dragon in me drive my therapeutic interventions. Sure I could still help her learn how to be more assertive and effective as a parent. However, I needed to first stop and slay the dragon of my *desire* for her to be safe so I could feel good. This may seem to be a subtle thing; for shouldn't a therapist do all he can to help someone? Yes, but if my comments are coming out of a tense body and anxious mind, the comments aren't helpful. Once I began to catch myself getting uptight, I would stop and breathe so that I could relax. The instant I was relaxed, I could then comment on how she might have handled the situation differently. She was able to hear and apply the suggestions when I was feeling relaxed and at peace. For when I was acting as if my feeling good and being at peace depended on her becoming assertive, she was shut down. She needed to have me relax and listen to her stories of being scared and intimidated by her son. She had been oppressed throughout her life: first by an intimidating father, then by an alcoholic husband, and now by a defiant son. She needed acceptance, compassion, and empathy from me before assertiveness training could take hold.

As I began to notice this pattern in my work with Jane, I suddenly saw how this pattern was underlying conflicts of all kinds. It was especially evident with couples and with parents and children.

So it was out of my experience with Jane and my observations of other patients that I sculpted the first four inner steps of S-T-O-P and the second four outer steps of L-O-V-E. I wanted to help myself and the people who saw me slay the dragon of dependency.

I also refer to the four steps of L-O-V-E as the left hand/right hand technique. On the one hand (left hand), we make room for the feelings, thoughts, opinions, point of view, etcetera, of the person with whom we are having a conflict. Once we slay the dragon with the four inner steps that spell STOP, we then proceed to the four outer steps. We L-listen with an O-open mind and heart as we V-validate by *verbalizing* back what the other person is saying.

Then, on the other hand (right hand), we E-express our feelings, thoughts, opinions, point of view, etcetera. When you E-express, you personalize your statements with I, me, and my rather than start with *you.* For example, you might say, "I feel upset that you ignored me," instead of saying, "You ignored me, and I'm upset." The former expresses, and the latter aggresses the stress you feel. Starting a statement with "You" tends to feel like an attack and puts the person on the defensive. Let's take a look at how you can practice the L-O-V (left hand stands for *listen*) AND E (right hand stands for assert your *rights*) steps of the left hand/right hand technique.

Practicing the Left Hand (L-O-V-) / Right Hand ((E) Technique

Angelina is a single parent with a teenage son. She has frequent battles over bed-time with her thirteen-year-old son Josh. In the morning, Angelina has her hands full getting Josh to wake up and get ready for school. Her first tactics were to cajole, plead, and over explain on the one hand. On the other, she would get frustrated and begin to raise her voice, threatening him with negative consequences where the punishment did not fit the crime. The threats were exaggerated, and she would not even attempt to enforce them.

She started to do the L-O-V-E steps. At Josh's first resistance to going to bed, Angelina would think of her left hand and say, "Honey, I know you'd rather stay up and watch TV, do video games, or listen to music."

Asserting her rights as a parent, she would think of her right hand and say, "Nevertheless, you need to get to bed within the next half hour so you can get up for school in the morning." She might add a few more left hand/right hand messages where she'd listen with an open mind and heart. And then she'd acknowledge and validate Josh's feelings. Then, on the other hand, she'd assert her parental authority. If necessary, she would coolly and calmly repeat the negative consequences of not getting up in the morning.

A husband seeing me for individual therapy complained that his wife saw his comments as debating; he saw what he was doing as discussing. Standing before a mirror, he practiced the left hand (LOV) / right hand (E) technique. He extended his left hand, and said, "To you I'm debating with you." Now extending his right hand, he said, "And to me, I'm discussing and exploring the topic."

Jordan was an attorney who had a big problem with procrastination until the deadline for acting drew nigh. She would wait until putting off taking action would be disastrous. She would anxiously anticipate approaching the people whose help she needed. On one particular occasion, Jordan came to see me upset that she had put off a preparing for a case; it was a case that she couldn't do without the help of a senior partner in her firm.

Jordan role played the dreaded situation of asking for help. She pictured the senior partner, extended her left hand and said, "I imagine you're upset and hate it that I waited so long before coming to see you. And that's because you would' have loved it if I had come to you months ago when I first knew I'd need your help."

Then, extending her right hand, she said, "And I'm upset with myself because I hate it that I waited so long since I couldn't face it. And that's because I would love it if I could have faced it and come to you when I first knew I was going to need your help."

• Stand before a mirror and practice the left hand messages (L-O-V) followed by right hand messages (E). Pick situations that will be coming up or ones that have already happened. First try the brief version. Extend your left hand from your heart as if to the other person, and say, "To you_____." Then gesture with your right hand saying, "And to me_____." Fill in the blanks with your concerns.

• Still looking in the mirror, extend your left hand and use the words, "You feel_____." Then extend your right hand and say, "And I feel_____." For example, a man seeing me was not sure how to respond to his wife's tendency to deprecate her appearance when they were going out. Practicing the left hand/right hand technique, he extended his left hand saying, "You feel you look fat in that dress." Now, extending his right hand, he said, "And I feel you look great in that dress." Then he might find a specific detail about the dress that he could use to compliment her such as, "I love how the color of the dress highlights your eyes."

• Practice helping others shift from a fear focus on what they *don't* want to a love focus on what they *do* want. The format is to look in the mirror and imagine a situation where a loved one, coworker or supervisor was upset. You could use an upcoming situation where you anticipate someone in your personal or professional life might get upset. Extend your left hand and say, "You're upset and hate it that_____. And that's *because* you would love it if_____." Then, extending your right hand, say, "And I'm upset and hate it that_____. And that's *because* I would love it if_____."

Using Left Hand/Right Hand to Resolve Inner Conflicts

Very often, couples find themselves polarized on various issues. In effect, one member of a couple would be for one pole of a conflict; and the other member would champion the opposite pole. Among the couples I saw there were the following dualities. One would be optimistic, the other pessimistic. One would be responsible, the other carefree. One would be tight with money, the other would pile up charges on their credit cards. One would see people as basically good, the other would see people as basically bad. One would be cynical and mistrusting, the other hopeful and trusting. One would be neat, the other messy.

In all cases, it was as if each member of a couple *specialized* in one pole of a conflict. In order to be more effective in the face of stress and conflict, we need to be more integrated and whole. We need to resolve the inner conflicts we all experience in confronting the divisive desires and dueling dualities of life.

For example, we all desire excitement *and* security. We need to stop externalizing our inner conflicting desires by projecting one set of desires onto our partner while we identify with the other set. As one woman told me, "I want to have fun, but my husband holds me back by telling me we have to be frugal." To stop battling, she and her husband had to see they both wanted to have fun *and* financial security. By using the left hand/right hand technique, e can start owning that we have both within us.

• What do you and your partner or friends fight over? What are you having conflicts over? Look in the mirror, or work with your partner. Take turns owning and accepting that you have the opposing desires within your heart. What do you and your partner get polarized over? Saving and spending? Closeness and distance? Dependency and independence? Extend your left hand from your heart and say, "On the one hand, I have a need and desire for closeness. I want to hold you and be held by you. I want to tell you about my hopes and dreams."

Then extend your right hand and say, "On the other hand, I

have a need and a desire for some time alone and separate from you."

Now your partner does the same and expresses the inner conflict in his or her own terms. "On the one hand, I need to feel close and intimate with you. And on the other hand, I need my space." Review some of the other polarities above and try owning and expressing each side to each other or by yourself looking in the mirror.

* * *

The focus for this week is on practicing L-listening. with an O-open heart and mind so that you can V-validate the feelings of the other person: your love partner, a friend, a colleague, your boss, your child. The important thing is to do whatever you need to do from the steps of S-T-O-P to get yourself relaxed so you can then listen before you express your feelings and opinions.

As the old saying goes, you first seek to understand and then to be understood. The dragon within you engages you in a reflexive, knee-jerk response to fight to express your feelings and opinions first. You are working on breaking this habit.

You are practicing the Golden Rule of doing unto others what you would have others do unto you. You would like others to listen to you with an open mind and heart; therefore you do that first for others. You are setting an example by exemplifying what you want others to do for you. And when you take your turn to speak, you have some *leverage* to assert your right to be heard. If the other person interrupts you, you can say, "Excuse me, it's my turn to speak. I listened to you, now I'd like you to listen to me."

Week Six

Validate the Hate & Link to Love

HELPING EACH OTHER REPLACE A FEAR FOCUS WITH A LOVE FOCUS

Weeding the Garden of Our Love

Our Love is like a garden we sow,
The safer we feel the more it can grow.

But if we are to achieve relationship bliss,
We truly must, simply must, remember this:

In such safe and fertile soil the flowers of love appear,
But right alongside sprout the weeds of our fear.

So let us weed out the fears of the past
So we can create a love that can last.

The flowers of our love will forever flourish,
And the depths of our souls we'll continually nourish.

BY PRACTICING THE FOUR OUTER STEPS OF L-O-V-E (the left hand/right hand technique), couples can help each other heal their hidden hurts. They can help each other release repressed pain over the common childhood and adolescent narcissistic (self-esteem) injuries: being humiliated, rejected, invalidated, discounted, belittled, made fun of, mocked, and misunderstood. I wrote the little poem above to convey the idea of how love partners can help each other blossom individually as they help their love relationship flourish. You can break down the process of weeding the garden of your love relationship into the following phases. If you are not currently in a love relationship, you can practice with a friend.

De-stressing versus Distressing Each Other

• Pick a place where you can sit face-to-face with your love partner. You are going to take turns expressing your stress from the day. When you are in the role of listening be sure to L-listen with an O-open mind and heart to what your partner is expressing. When you speak, you V-validate the feelings of your partner. You do this by verbalizing what you hear and understand your partner to be expressing.

• While in the role of listener, you do not E-express any of your suggestions for solutions. You just stay focused on listening and clarifying your partner's concerns. Spend at least five minutes listening before switching roles. You can set a time limit you are both comfortable with. If one of you had a particularly stressful day, then you two may decide the stressed person needs more time.

• Validating is not a simple parroting back words you hear. Instead, you express your *understanding* which may include *unstated* undercurrents. For example, let's say your partner is sounding angry about a situation at work. However, you pick up some fear under the anger.

> You first reflect back the anger, and then you comment on the underlying fear. "You're angry at your boss for how he is handling this situation, and you sound afraid that he might fire you. And that's why you're ready to fight for him to hear what your position is on the situation."

Validating the Hate & Shifting to a Love Focus

Validating the hate involves verbalizing back what you hear your partner saying by using the shift your focus and energy technique. For example, let's say your spouse is upset about your ten-year-old son being suspended from school for fighting.

Your spouse has mixed feelings because your son was defending himself. But because there is a zero-tolerance policy for fights at school, both parties in a fight get disciplined. Your spouse says, "I'm so upset that he is suspended. And yet I wouldn't want him to get picked on and not feel he can defend himself. I have such mixed feelings about the whole thing."

You validate the hate to help your spouse shift from a fear focus to a love focus by saying, "You're upset and hate it that he was in a fight, was suspended and will miss schoolwork. And you'd love it if he didn't have to miss school. But if he had to be in a fight, you're glad he didn't start it, and you're glad that he stood up for himself. You'd love it if he wasn't penalized for standing up for himself."

Validating the Hate & Using the Look Through Technique

You and your partner may decide to practice weeding the garden of your love so that your love can grow and deepen. And by weeding the garden, as the poem suggests, you can grow as individuals as well. You grow by identifying and pulling out the weeds of your fears which include hurts, and disappointments from your past.

When we fall in love, we are unconsciously finding in our partner someone who is similar to the first people we loved: parents, siblings, grandparents, aunts, uncles, etcetera. The conflicts we had with these first people will inevitably resurface by breaking through the soil of our garden of love. Agreeing to do a daily de-stressing versus distressing of each other can help you weed the garden of your love. And it can help each of you weed the garden of your individual souls as well. Remember, your *partner* is not your *parent*.

Remember, repeated relationship stress not only occurs with your partner, it can occur with other emotionally-significant people in your life: your boss, your colleagues, and your children.

When the Stress is with Your Partner

Ben was furious with his wife Jennifer. He began his de-stressing by saying, "I really feel angry with your condescending and controlling attitude when you tell me what to do, how I should feel, and what I should wear. I really get mad when you correct my comments. It's like I can't do anything right in your eyes. Right now you have that arched eyebrow that makes you look haughty to me. I feel you are looking at me disapprovingly, as though my anger is not justified. You make me feel like I am a little boy."

"You are upset with me," Jennifer reflected, "because you feel I am looking down at you. And you feel that I am trying to control you. I am getting the impression that you feel I am trying to correct you, even mold you."

"Yes, that's right," Ben said. "You are always trying to improve me!" Ben shouted, his face showing a noticeable relief.

"Your frustration with me," Jennifer said, "is telling you that you *hate* how critical and controlling I can be. And that's because you'd love it if I were more accepting and understanding."

"Absolutely!." Ben affirmed. "And I'd love it if you would be more appreciative of what I do *well,* and tell me. And I'd love it if your criticisms could be more constructive."

"In accord with our agreement to help each other heal the hidden hurts of the past," said Jennifer, "try *looking through* me and see the person in your family when you were growing up to whom you could say the words that you said to me about what you hate."

Ben saw both of his parents, but mostly his father. Then Jennifer asked him how old he was the first time he felt this way. The first age that came to mind for Ben was six years old.

Ben began addressing his father, "I hate how you criticize and control me. And that's because I'd love it if you noticed what I do well. I hate how you want to change and correct me. And that's because I'd love it if you would accept me."

Ben recalled other ages when he had something to say to his father. When Ben could think of no more ages and incidents, Jennifer encouraged him to hug his younger selves into his heart. He could now feel empowered to coolly and calmly express to

Jennifer what he couldn't express to his parents as a child.

Then Ben said to Jennifer, "Now that you know how I feel when you criticize and try to control me, can you look through me and see the person in your family when you were growing up who was critical and controlling of you, and made you feel the way I feel?"

Jennifer looked through and saw her mother. And the first age she recalled feeling scolded and criticized was seven. She told Ben the following story. She had come home from school. There had been a spelling test in school that day and Jennifer got one word wrong. Her mother didn't praise her for what she did right. Her mother launched into a tirade shouting, "How could you get this word wrong?! We went over it!"

Jennifer couldn't even remember the word despite how her mother kept repeating and spelling it over and over. Again and again. She recalled her mother did this for what seemed like an hour. With tears forming in her eyes, Jennifer remembered crying in her room.

Ben encouraged Jennifer to stand up to her mother in that scene. "I hated how you criticized me. And that's because I'd have loved it if you could have appreciated and praised me for the words I got right. I hate it that you didn't even think of how disappointed I was before you heaped your disappointment and anger on me. And that's because I'd have loved it if you would have comforted and encouraged me by saying something like, "I know you would have loved to get all the words correct, but you did well, Honey. You can try to get all the words right on the next test."

Ben asked Jennifer to see if there were other ages when she had something to say. There were. She did as before: she stood up to her mother, and told her what she hated and would have loved instead. She hugged her younger selves back into her heart. Then she tearfully told Ben she was sorry for *doing* to him what was *done* to her. She resolved to be constructive in her criticism and asked Ben to help her by calling her on the pattern she'd been locked into.

Standing up to the mother in her *memory* really helped Jennifer. It is in standing up to the parent in your psyche that you find your freedom. You are mentally and emotionally shaking yourself loose of the patterns interfering with your adult happiness. This *inner* confrontation with your personal emotional history helps to set you free to be the person you want to be instead of staying stuck like a caged rat running on the wheel of childhood conditioning.

The Destructive Weed of Control & Criticism

The critical and controlling weed in the garden of your love relationship as well as in the garden of your soul can choke off the flowers of love. It is vitally important to confront the dragon's controlling tendency in yourself and to help your partner do the same.

Our early experiences of the hierarchical relationship of parent/child leave their mark on us. How our parents handled this difference in power leads to two extreme roles when stress strikes later in life. Victim or victimizer.

Critical parents who levied harsh, unloving criticism at their child hurt their child's self-esteem. As an adult, the harshly criticized child is highly sensitive to criticism on the one hand. And yet, on the other hand, he or she can be *unmercifully* critical of others. The critical person is unconsciously getting revenge by doing to others what the critical person's parents did to him or her.

If your parents reacted with contempt and disgust when you didn't understand something, then you will be at risk for reacting the same way. You are likely to react with contempt and disgust when your partner and other people don't understand something or when they make a mistake. If you were made to feel stupid when you were small and helpless, then you are likely to reverse roles and look down on others, thinking of them, even calling them, stupid.

But if you remember how hurt you felt then you may make a conscious effort to counter treating others as you were treated. You and your partner can help each other develop acceptance, compassion and empathy for the child each of you once was. You will help your love flourish as you also have empathy for each other's personal emotional histories and the hurts you suffered.

Unless we remember how we felt hurt as a child, whenever we

feel stress, we may react in the child role of powerless-persecuted victim; or we may reverse the role and be the powerful-persecuting parent. This is what is happening when you or your partner become critical, scolding, attacking, invalidating, discounting, belittling, mocking, and so forth.

Certainly, it can feel better to have power than to feel powerless. This shift happens unconsciously in an effort to not be hurt as an adult as we were as a child. It can happen so automatically that you or your partner do not realize this reversal of childhood roles is happening. Victim grows up to become victimizer.

$$* * *$$

The focus for this week is on you and your partner practicing de-stressing versus distressing. Again, you can do this with a friend. You can do it alone if need be. You just focus on expressing what you hated and would have loved instead. The important thing is for you to weed the garden of your soul by doing the look through technique.

Validating the hate and then linking the *intensity* of the hate to love puts more passion into your life. And when the hate you feel is in your love relationship, you inject more passion into your love life as well. "I hate how you rarely make eye contact with me when we talk," a wife says to her husband. "And that's because I love it when you look into my eyes with those gorgeous eyes of yours," she continues. She feels her passion for her husband, and he feels her passion for him as well. She only hates the lack of eye contact *because* she would so love to have more eye contact.

If you are in a love relationship be sure that you both agree to use the look through. And do not use it as a way to shift the heat off yourself. It wasn't *just* that Jennifer reminded Ben of his mother. Jennifer was critical, and she stood to benefit by making some changes. Of course, we all have sensitive areas based on our personal emotional history, and we need to be sensitive to each other's wounded areas. Then we can help each other heal the hidden hurts interfering with our present happiness.

Week Seven

When You Want to Attack

LISTENING BY MIRRORING WHEN YOU HAVE AN URGE TO ATTACK

Do you ever feel like screaming any of the following in response to something someone says that you totally disagree with? "You're an idiot if that's what you think! That's completely absurd! How can you think that!" Did you have aggressive fantasies of verbally or physically attacking the person frustrating you? If so, you were being driven by the dragon in you.

The problem with a direct attack on the person you're frustrated with is that it puts the person on the defensive. Communication degenerates into the dragon in us breathing fire. Nothing is accomplished. Anger rules the interaction, precluding effective communication and the resolving of conflict.

Think about what it is you would *really* love to have happen when you feel someone is being ridiculous, absurd, or off-the-wall in his or her comments. What would really make you feel good?

After delving into that question myself, I concluded that I really wanted the person to *see* and therefore *feel* the absurd implications of what he or she was saying. As you will see in the examples I give, I realized my instinctive fire-breathing-dragon response was not going to accomplish that goal. It would only drive the person into a defensive position. This would not help me *show* and *tell* the person of the impact he or she was having on me and others.

On several occasions, in dealing with domestic violence, I had fantasies of verbally, and in one instance physically, attacking the abusive member of the couple consulting me. Sometimes the abusive member was the woman. Yes. I had seen couples where the guy was verbally *and* physically beaten by his wife. Not because he was a wimp. In most cases, the men were brawny and refused to strike a woman. These men would walk away from the fight as the women beat on them.

"I didn't hit you. I didn't use my fist. I pushed you with my forearm like this." Ted was making a distinction between shoving and hitting his wife. Under my cool professional exterior, I was seething. I was seized by the dragon's urge to attack. I imagined shouting. *Hey, buddy! Wake up! Hitting. Shoving. Neither are acceptable in a so-called love relationship.*

Nevertheless, there was a moment in my office when I was challenged to practice what I preach. Filled with the rage of the fire-breathing dragon, I resorted to the four outer steps. In the heat of this clinical moment, the wisdom of my unconscious mind gave me an apt image involving me, the abuser, and a mirror: it helped me clarify how we can handle such situations. We act as a mirror.

Left Hand/Right Hand Mirroring: A Case of Domestic Violence

Martin had been accused of raping and beating his wife Betty. He was on probation and came to see me for individual therapy. Betty had left him, and she took their young son with her. She sought refuge by moving back to her family in a neighboring state.

I am going to go into more detail to describe what took place in the sessions and within me than I did when I discussed this case in *8 Steps to Love.* I want to show you how you *can* convert the urge to attack into compassionate listening by mirroring instead of attacking. Sometimes people make absurd claims, and the instinct is to confront and attack the absurd statement(s) directly. All this tends to accomplish is to drive their defenses up, and shore up their position.

After a month of seeing me, Martin asked if I thought his wife Betty could return home. He seemed to have made progress. She called me and returned home with the understanding that she and

Martin would be coming in for marital therapy. For three sessions at the rate of one per week, we had focused on practicing the four steps for relieving conflict: L-listen, O-open, V-validate, and E-express. They seemed to be getting the hang of it and were communicating better.

In the second session, Martin interrupted Betty because she had failed to validate what he had said *before* expressing her feelings. He raised his voice, and, with an urgency behind his words, he said, "Repeat what I said! Repeat what I said!" Not exactly what I had in mind. However, Betty stopped what she was saying to state her understanding of what he had said. He was relieved. I could sense the ignored and invalidated little boy in Martin the man.

Later in the second session, I could see Martin's well-hidden anger starting to surface. He said, "We're not going to be friends with those neighbors anymore. It's because of them that I am saddled with thousands of dollars in attorney fees."

Well, yeah, that's true—in a logical causal sense. Your neighbors did call the police, I thought *But what about your behavior?!* I shouted in my head, the dormant dragon in me beginning to stir. But it was in the next session that I had to gather all my emotional strength to slay the dragon in me with the sword of L-O-V-E.

Martin started the third session with a statement that shocked and infuriated me. In the first session, we had gone over the horrid events that led to Betty leaving. Martin and Betty had discussed the details of the assault and rape. Both agreed on what had happened, and Martin was sorry for his actions. Then, referring to the incident, he blurted out, "By the way, I didn't rape you!"

A fantasy flashed in my mind as I felt my back and shoulder muscles tense. At the same instant, I felt the heat of the dragon's fire blaze under my collar. I imagined getting up from my seat, grabbing Martin by the scruff of his neck, and lifting him from his chair. Then I saw myself repeatedly bash his face into the large Victorian mirror with a thick-gilded-gold frame over my fireplace. I imagined his nose bled and bloodied the mirror. He was not a small man—we were about the same size.

Half-formed thoughts followed the rage-driven fantasy. I couldn't believe what I was hearing him say. I thought, *We went over your heinous actions in our first session. How can you sit there and deny what you admitted to in our first marital session?!*

I then thought, *My God, you're going to blow it and alienate your wife!* Next, I imagined saying something with the words and tone of detective Andy Sipowitz (Dennis Franz) on the popular TV series at that time, N.Y.P.D. Blue. *Get out of my office, you scum of the earth! I'm in private practice. I don't have to work with someone like you. Go to a clinic!*

Finally, the fire in my heart began to die down to a few glowing embers. I looked at Betty and the warm glow of compassion filled my heart. No more traces of the dragon's fire. *My God, this poor woman . . . I have to help her. After all I'm responsible for her coming home. I gave her the green light, and said I believed it was safe for her to return.* Then, I looked at him and thought, *Somebody has to help him, too. And it might as well be me.* My fantasy and the thoughts that followed, all happened in the blur of microseconds.

First, from my left hand, I followed the first three steps of L-listening with an O-open mind and heart, and V-validating by verbalizing what I was hearing. I leaned forward and looked Martin straight in the eye saying, "Let me see if I understand what you're saying. You are saying that when you grabbed your wife's face, yelled you f---ing bitch, tore her nightgown off, and forced yourself on her, for you that wasn't rape?"

Before I delivered these words coolly and calmly, I felt my anger subside some as I had a fantasy of doing my Jack Nicholson impression. I imagined saying the words I said in the tone of voice Nicholson used as Randall McMurphy in *One Flew Over the Cuckoo's Nest.* And I imagined adding, *Can you help me understand just what in the hell that was if it wasn't rape?!*

I sensed that this question would have ben too much even if I refrained from asking it as McMurphy would. No matter how professionally I may have asked the question, it would have pushed Martin over the edge. He already looked stunned; it was as though his brain shut down. I imagined his brain went *boing,* sending springs out of his head and smoke out of his ears.

I took the last step of E-expressing my position from my right hand. With my eyes still fixed on Martin's eyes, I said, "As three adults here, I think we can assume that whatever you call it, it's totally unacceptable behavior, especially in a loving relationship, so let's move on." We did. As of my last contact with them, they were happier and they were successfully using the steps of L-O-V-E.

A Humorous Example of Left Hand/Right Hand Mirroring

Let's consider a humorous example of mirroring from an episode of the widely acclaimed 1990's hit TV series *Seinfeld.* Jerry Seinfeld and his friend George are sitting in the coffee shop they frequent. Jerry is listening to George. George is expressing his indignation about what had just happened at the birthday party for his girlfriend's young son.

At the party, George saw smoke coming from the kitchen area. George panicked and shouted, "Fire!" George raced out of the building knocking down children and a lady on a walker. It turned out there was no fire, just something burning on the stove. George's girlfriend was upset with him.

In expressing his indignation to Jerry, George feels that his girlfriend should have appreciated what he did. He claims to be a hero leading the way for others to follow. And, he thinks he should be commended since he didn't discriminate. Instead of a policy of women and children exiting first, he champions a kind of non-discriminating, equal-opportunity policy.

From the left hand (L-O-V), Jerry mirrors the absurdity instead of verbally attacking George. "So, basically, it's every man, woman, child, and invalid for themselves." George responds by saying, "She [his girlfriend] should be proud of me for treating everyone like equals."

Jerry responds by commenting on George's girlfriend. From the right hand, Jerry E-expresses his position by saying, "Well, perhaps when she's released from the burn center, she'll see things clearly." In the confusion, George's girlfriend burned her hand on the stove. Now Jerry's comment picks up on an absurd implication of what George is saying. But it does border on sarcasm which is ultimately going to fuel conflict. It doesn't in this case since George seems to feel mirrored, not mocked

As tempting as it may be to say something sarcastic, try to stick with verbalizing the absurd implications of what he or she is saying as Jerry does. Mirror. Don't mock.

Practicing Mirroring: L-O-V (Left Hand) & E (Right Hand)

• Deepen your compassion by focusing on the step of O-opening your mind and heart to the person saying something that angers you and appears absurd. Practice silently saying the mantra of compassion. "I know in my heart that you would have reacted differently if you could have but you couldn't so you didn't."

You can feel compassion for how the person—your love partner, boss, friend, relative, etcetera—is still stuck with alienating and ineffective ways of responding to stress.

• Practice listening when you strongly disagree with what the other person is saying. In fact, open your mind and heart to the possibility that what may seem absurd to you might not be from the other person's point of view.

Don't assume you are right and the other person is off-the-wall. Give the person a chance to express his or her position and validate it by verbalizing what you understand the person to be saying. You may be surprised that the person's position actually makes sense when you look at the situation from his or her frame of reference.

• Remember, it is important to avoid lapsing into sarcasm. Really listen with an open mind and heart before you verbalize back what you believe you are hearing.

• Listening by holding up a mirror and validating the hate instead of launching a counterattack applies not only to conflicts with loved ones but to conflicts at work.

Let's take a conflict with a boss. Imagine you have a boss who is upset with you not getting a project done on time. You first listen before you defend yourself and express how you feel. Given the obstacles that got in the way of completing the project on time, you strongly feel it is absurd for the boss to come down on you. However, the boss may not have been informed of the obstacles.

On the left hand, you do steps L-O-V by saying, "You're upset with my performance and you hate how I went over the deadline." Then from your right hand, you do step E by expressing your position, "I understand how you are upset. I am upset, too. I hate it that I didn't meet the deadline. However, there were obstacles that were totally unexpected and beyond my control. I'm not making excuses. I just want to set the record straight."

You then go on to help the boss understand just what the obstacles were. You don't make excuses. You give a detailed explanation to *show* the absurdity of expecting the deadline to be met. If necessary, you might mirror the absurdity by saying to the boss, "So you feel that I should still have met the deadline despite these unforeseen events that made it humanly impossible to do so?"

* * *

The focus for this week is on practicing listening when the dragon in you wants to breathe fire. You practice listening when you have a strong urge to defend yourself or attack the other person's position. Remember. Mirror. Don't mock.

You first need to notice that you have a desire to verbally and/or physically attack the other person. You stop the dragon in its tracks by taking slow-deep-belly breaths. Your breathing helps you enter the dragon's cave and make space so the fantasies can unfold.

Then, you convert the fantasies into holding up the mirror. You reflect back the absurdity and contradictions that you are hearing. You can include the implications of what the other person is saying.

Keep your mind and heart open to the possibility that what the other person is saying may make sense and *not* be absurd. You just L-listen with an O-open mind and heart to the other person's point of view. Be prepared to be surprised. I have been surprised on many occasions when I truly listened with an open mind and heart.

Week Eight
Expressing by Demonstrating

EXPRESS & DEMONSTRATE WHAT YOU WANT

"ARE YOU GOING TO SETTLE ON A SHOW OR NOT! It's almost five minutes past nine!" Bob growled. His wife Pam had the TV remote. It was five minutes past the hour and most shows were getting started. Bob wanted to pick one. Pam responded with, "It wasn't necessary to say it like that! All you had to say was, 'Honey, it is getting past the hour, could you pick a show for us to watch?'"

This simple exchange packed the punch of a powerful insight for me: don't even describe what you don't want, and demonstrate what you do want. Don't dwell on what you don't want, and don't even dignify it with a description. What a stunningly simple idea! Demonstrate what you would love to have happen. Express and demonstrate the tone of voice and the words you would rather have heard.

When Bob and Pam related the experience, I thought about how often people *overreact*. They don't express what they would love to have happen until they are boiling inside. And then what spews forth regarding the person's negative behavior scalds the person.

People, especially men, may use a cannon when a water pistol would do. Bob shared how it was as if a light went on in a pitch-dark room. "You mean I can say something softly and it would be heard? Wow." This simple incident made me think of how demonstrating what we would love instead can be very helpful. It is all part of sustaining the love focus on desired outcomes, on what we *do* want instead of dwelling on what we *don't* want.

As a corollary to this insight, I added the idea of using the don't want as a springboard to what we do want. So often, people complain: "You never listen. You always ignore what I say. You are always late. You're never on time." The focus is on what we don't want; we nail the other person to the cross of his or her shortcomings. The person's focus is fixed on what is wrong with him or her.

Pam didn't complain about or even go into describing the undesirable behavior. She said, "You didn't have to say it like that." There is no *derogatory description* or *mocking imitation*. She didn't say something like, "You don't have to yell and be mean." Inevitably, we can imagine the knee-jerk response to be, "I didn't yell. I wasn't being mean!" And we're off to the races of argument. He defends himself. She counters. And on it goes.

Since there is great energy in the don't want, we can use it to put the emphasis and focus on what we'd love to have happen. When I would ask people in therapy what they wanted, they would often draw a blank. But if I asked them, "What bothers you? What is it that you don't want?" Instantly, they had an answer.

So fill in the blanks. Focus on specific things that the other person *says* or *does*. "I hate it when you_____. And that's because I'd love it if you would_____."

"It upsets me when you_____. And that's because I'd love it if you would_____."

"It hurts me when you_____. And that's because I'd love it if you would_____."

Dealing with Someone Attacking You with Absolute Claims

"You never listen! You always have to have it your way! You never admit you're wrong! You always have to be right!" So in response to such claims, you can try saying something like the following:

"It's not necessary to express yourself to me like that to get your point across to me. All you have to do is say, "I'm upset about _____. And I wish you would_____."

Golden Rule of Assertiveness

Do unto others what you would have others do unto you, if you behaved as badly as they. Let's say someone cuts in line ahead of you at the movie theater. The idea is to say and do something that *you* would feel was fair for someone to say and do to you, if you cut in line as that person just did.

You temper your reaction by imagining you behaved as badly. Would you find it acceptable for someone to yell at you? Or would you feel that a tap on the shoulder and a comment like, "Excuse me, you just cut in line, could you please go to the end of the line and wait just like the rest of us?" The idea is to put yourself in the person's place. Determine how assertive you would be comfortable with the person being toward you if you behaved as badly as he or she just did. Apply the rule by reviewing past instances of rude and inconsiderate words and actions that you have witnessed.

Show and Tell Them: Practicing Expressing What You Want

A Wife Shows & Tells her Husband

Ray, a thirty-one-year-old man, is always interrupting his wife Jane when she gets upset. He rushes in to fix the problem. He wants to rescue her with what he believes are his invaluable insights. However, when people are in the grip of their strong emotions, they need to release their painful feelings first. After that, you can help others look at the situation they are upset about. Ray really tries to talk Jane out of feeling as she does. She resents this.

Jane coolly and calmly tells Ray, "Instead of giving me advice right away, I'd love it if you would just listen until I can calm down." Keeping her voice soft, Jane says, "I'm upset about what's happening at work. And I wish you would just hear what is bothering me before you give me any suggestions. I just need you to comfort me first by letting me know you can see what I am dealing with. All you have to say is something like, 'Wow, Honey, that really is a pain. I'm sorry you have to go through that.'"

A Husband Shows & Tells His Wife

April, a woman in her mid-thirties, yells at her husband John, "You never listen!" April slams her hand down on the kitchen counter, rattling the pile of plates.

Usually, John defends himself by shouting back, "I always listen!" Instead, he takes a slow-deep-belly breath and calmly states, "It's not necessary to express yourself like that to get your point across to me. All you have to do is say, 'I'm upset about _____. And I wish you would_____.'" John demonstrates—shows and tells—by his relaxed tone of voice *how* he would like her to speak to him. John then adds, "I'm ready to listen."

A Distraught Mother Shows & Tells Her Adult Daughter

At thirty-three years old, Sue is still living at home. Sue often yells at her mother Pat, blaming her for everything that's wrong. Sue is in a hostile-dependent relationship with her mother. Sue is having one of her raging, shouting spells. Pat takes a slow-deep-belly breath, and calmly says, "It's not necessary to express yourself like that to get your point across to me. All you have to do is say, 'I'm upset about _____. And I wish you would_____.'" Pat demonstrates with a relaxed body and a calm tone of voice how she would like Sue to address her.

Sue continues to shout. So Pat silently does her cools and calms and says firmly and calmly, "I'm ready to listen as soon as you can talk to me instead of shouting and banging things. We can talk later when you are calmer." When Pat sees that Sue is not going to calm down, she leaves the room saying, "I'll be glad to listen when you are ready to talk and not shout."

Pat goes into her home office, and she shuts and locks the door. Sue follows and starts banging on the door. Pat firmly states, "When you can stop shouting, and say something like, 'Mom, I really need to talk. I promise I won't start shouting,' then we can talk." Sue stops and walks away. She comes back in five minutes and asks to talk. If Sue kept up the banging, Pat was prepared to warn Sue that she'd call the police if Sue didn't stop her verbally and physically threatening behavior.

Pat had coddled Sue since Sue was a toddler and her father left. It was as if there was a toddler in Sue's adult body crying out for limits. Pat didn't provide boundaries for Sue to bump up against. With no external limits, the child has difficulty developing internal controls. So Sue had never developed the inner control of self-talk that would help regulate and modulate her emotions and actions.

A Woman Shows & Tells Her Roommate

Terri's roommate Joey is beyond fastidious. However, what really upsets Terri is how unaware Joey is of his own messiness, but is quick to point out and pounce on the messiness of others.

First, Terri realizes by looking through Joey that he is reminding her of her truly wicked stepmother. Once she sees this, she is less intense in her anger. Terri shows and tells Joey. "It wasn't necessary to react as strongly as you did regarding the crumbs on the kitchen counter. I clean up after you and your friends when you leave dishes in the sink late at night, and I find them in the morning. I'm glad to do it. I'd like you to do the same for me regarding any mess I make and happen to miss."

Terri continues by demonstrating with her choice of words and tone of voice what she'd like to hear from Joey. "If you must say something then a gentle reminder will do. For example, you might say something like, 'Terri, I found some crumbs on the counter this morning. Please try to keep the counter clean.'"

* * *

The focus for this week is on practicing E-expressing what you want. Show and tell others how they could be more *effective* when it comes to you. Practice demonstrating what you would love to have happen. Be sure to demonstrate by using the tone of voice, wording, and actions that you would prefer. Keep your body relaxed as you demonstrate what you want.

III
Aspiring to Mastery

Week Nine

Practicing All 8 Steps

APPLYING ALL 8 STEPS IN THE HEAT OF THE MOMENT

WHEN THE DRAGON REARS ITS UGLY HEAD IN THE stress of conflict with another person, we can apply the four inner steps of S-T-O-P in an instant. Then we focus most of our efforts on applying the four outer steps. Often we just take a breath, relax and go right to the four outer steps of L-O-V-E.

Often we may wait until later to do the emotional step of looking through the present to the past hurt. However, we may actually be able to do that very quickly in the moment as well.

Sometimes you simply identify the stress as one you are aware of and are working on. "Ah, there's my anger over not feeling understood," you might say. Later on when you are alone or when you are *de-stressing* your day with your partner, you might look through the present to the past. Below are some examples of how you can apply the steps in the heat of conflict.

Applying the 8 Steps to the Stress of Being Criticized

David was sensitive to criticism. In fact, he had just begun to see how his whole life was organized around avoiding a core concern: being criticized. He strove to do things so perfectly that he would never get criticized. He harbored a hidden hurt of being criticized and picked on by his perfectionistic parents. Consequently, David felt compelled to do whatever he could to avoid reexperiencing the early hurt he felt as a helpless child.

Sometimes he would engage in self-defeating actions. He would defend himself and never admit mistakes. When his wife found fault with him, he'd fly off into a moment of rage. On this particular occasion, David's boss had criticized his performance on a project he was in charge of as chief engineer.

"This project has not turned out as I had expected," the boss said, bemoaning the outcome of David's work. David felt the hair bristle on the back of his neck. He felt his face flush red with rage: he was infuriated. And he could feel a tsunami of anger threatening to wash away his capacity to reason. His shoulder muscles tensed and his jaw tightened; he was fighting the compelling urge to launch into a defensive tirade. Instead, he S-stopped himself and did some slow-deep-belly breaths, standing there before his boss who was seated at his desk. He told himself, "I can keep my mind cool . . ." then exhaling, he thought, "and my body calm no matter what!"

David started to shift his focus and energy from a fear focus that was fueling his anger to a love focus. He began to T-tell himself, "My rage is telling me that I hate it when you or anyone finds fault with me. And that's because I'd love it if you would never find fault with me and always appreciate my efforts." Of course, at some level of awareness, David knew this was an impossible goal. Still, that was the truth he held in his heart: "I *never* want to be criticized. I want to be above reproach."

David O-observed and faced the truth of the stress gap of being criticized and never wanting to be criticized. And he felt how familiar this anger at being criticized was. But he needed to do the steps of L-O-V-E with his boss right now. He'd explore the hidden hurt later. So he proceeded to breathe slowly and deeply as he listened. He told himself as he inhaled, "Breathing in cool, I remind myself that I can keep my cool, feel good, and be at peace as I let you express your criticism." Then, as he exhaled, he told himself, "Breathing out calm, I know in my heart I did a good job and I'll explain what happened after you [his boss] states his concerns."

David V-validated the concerns of his boss by verbalizing back what he understood the boss to be saying. "So you believe that I did not manage and motivate my men on this project. And you strongly believe we not only could have done it better, but we could have done it more quickly and more efficiently." David clarified and crystallized the criticisms of his boss.

Once it was clear that the boss was finished, David said, "I understand your concerns. Now I'd like to explain the problems we were dealing with that I did not want to bother you with. I can see now that I should have told you about the problem I was having with getting parts from our distributor." David went on to detail what led to the delay and the lack of efficiency. From his left hand, he let his boss know, "I was wrong to not inform you of the problems my men and I were facing." From his right hand, he said, "I really thought I could handle it without complaining to you. You have so many other things on your plate." Using more left hand/right hand messages, David resolved the issue with his boss .

That night, David took some time in his study at home. He relaxed himself and recalled his rage when the boss first criticized him. He reenacted the moment by saying aloud, "My rage is telling me that I hate it when you or anyone criticizes me. And that's because I'd love it if I were never criticized. I hate it when you or anyone finds fault with what I do. And that's because I'd love it if I never made mistakes and could always be perfect in your eyes."

Again, David O-observed the familiarity of the feeling. He looked through the situation with his boss and saw how he could say the same kind of thing to his father and mother. He imagined saying to his parents, "I hate how you always find fault with me. And that's because I'd love it if you'd appreciate and praise me for what I do right."

David saw himself as eight years old. He recalled how his father criticized David's homework. David continued, "I hate how you and Mom were so *hard* on me. And that's because I'd have loved it if you and Mom could have been kinder and more constructive in your criticism. I hate how I'm as hard on myself as you and Mom were. And that's because I'd love to be easier on myself. I now resolve to still strive for excellence, but I will *not* beat myself up verbally when I make a mistake. Only God is perfect."

Then David returned his focus to the present as he imagined hugging into his heart his hurt eight-year-old self. He resolved to be more realistic in his pursuit of excellence. He resolved to ask his boss and others for help rather than try to do it all himself. When he finished, David went to his wife with tears in his eyes and shared his insight. He apologized for all the times he had been angry when she pointed out a mistake or problem. David was ready to take off his protective suit of perfectionistic armor. It was not so bad to admit mistakes; he was not that helpless child trying so hard to keep the heat of his parents' relentless scrutiny from scorching him.

Hometown Hero Applies the 8 Steps to Stress with the Press

Don was a hometown hero returning to his hometown after many years. He had been a star baseball player who had played in the majors. He had been a bonus baby: a super pitcher who was also a home-run hitter. In high school he had pitched a no hitter and hit the home run that was the only run scored. His team had won by that one run. It was now twenty-five years since he had been back to his hometown. He was still considered a legend.

Don had been on a lecture tour since leaving professional baseball. He had recently published a book and was in his hometown for a book signing. When his signing was poorly attended, Don was upset. He was alternating between anger and sadness. He had consulted me for help with transitioning back to ordinary life after being in the blazing glory of the big leagues. He was doing well until this cold reception in his hometown. He was riding in the cab back to the airport, seething on the one hand, and, feeling sad on the other. He had his cell phone in hand and was about to call the local paper and give someone hell for not getting the press release out. Then he told me he did the 8 steps.

First, he S-stopped himself from calling the local newspaper. Then he silently yelled, "STOP!" He did slow-deep-belly breathing and he told himself as he inhaled, "Breathing in cool, I stop and still my mind." Then, as he exhaled, he silently said, "Breathing out calm, I stop and still my body." Then, as he inhaled, he reminded himself, "I can keep my mind cool . . ." and then as he exhaled he silently said, "and my body calm no matter what!"

Don began to T-tell himself, "My anger at you, my hometown press, is telling me that I hate it that you ignored my homecoming—after all I'm one of your own. And that's because I'd love it if you paid attention to me and were proud of my accomplishments."

The instant the words came into his mind, Don O-observed how familiar the feeling of being ignored was. He looked through the press reporters, and he saw that he could say similar words to his parents when he was little. He imagined saying, "My anger and sadness are telling me that I hate it that I'm your own, and you ignore me and don't let me know how proud you are of me. And that's because I'd love it if you expressed how you were proud of me and my accomplishments."

As soon as Don saw where his anger and sadness were coming from, he P-proceeded to call his hometown newspaper. He could do so coolly and calmly and not feel like a frustrated and helplessly enraged little boy. He could now be an adult who had a right to inquire into the huge oversight. He knew there were probably many people who would like to read his book. He wanted to talk to someone who could write an article about his book in the newspaper.

Instantly, he stopped himself from being driven by the dragon and the hurt child riding on the back of the beast. We are in real danger of serious aggression, once the hurt child in us saddles up the dragon and holds the reins. Don had released the reins from the grip of the hurt child in himself, and he was able to be firm without anger in his voice. He began to use the steps of L-O-V-E as soon as he started to feel some residual anger. He chose to *express* rather than aggress his stress by attacking in anger. He said to the head sportswriter, "Help me understand what happened. I am one of your hometown boys who made it in the big leagues, and yet not a word was printed about my homecoming and book signing. There are a lot of people who would like to know about my book."

The head sportswriter was apologetic and said that he had been out sick, and his staff had dropped the ball. They were younger and didn't remember Don as the head sportswriter had. Still, he conveyed to Don that there was no good reason for this to have happened. He promised Don that he would personally write an article about the book that included a public admission of the unforgivable oversight.

For some reason, Don did not feel as good as he thought he would after talking with the sportswriter. He then P-proceeded to do the other part of the spiritual step. He took a slow-deep-belly breath and prayed saying, "Please help me see this situation in a new light so that I can . . ." He paused, exhaled and continued his prayer, "let go of my anger and sadness, feel better, find peace and resolution." Then Don remembered the game of pennies from heaven. He took the change he had in his pocket and found one penny among some quarters, nickels, and dimes. He noticed the date was 1990. What was the significance of that date? Then it hit him. That was the year his father died.

Don's father had been dead for ten years. Both of Don's parents had been of the generation that thought complimenting a child would spoil him. But what was hitting Don was that he had never expressed to his father his hurt, anger, and sadness that his father had never told him that he was proud of Don's accomplishments. This left Don feeling empty inside; and the press ignoring his homecoming had ripped open the old wound, the hidden hurt of Don's past.

That night in his hotel room, Don visualized his father sitting in an empty chair. Don spoke out loud. Tears streamed down his cheeks. Using his left hand and right hand, Don said, "Dad, I understand the generation you came from that believed it was bad to praise kids. However, to this day, it really hurts and angers me that you never said, 'Son I'm proud of you.'"

Don then called his wife and shared what had happened. Her listening with an open heart and mind, and validating his feelings made Don feel much better. He had taken a big step toward healing this hidden hurt of his past. He thanked God for the message that came through the penny: the year of his father's death. Not the year his mother died. Sure Don wanted to hear that his mother was proud of him, too. The difference was that his mother's eyes told him she was proud of him. This didn't hold for his father whose stoic, poker face hid any trace of being pleased.

A Mother Applies the 8 Steps to Stress with Her Teenage Son

Anne's teenage son Brad could really set her off. She saw him as gifted and was bending over backwards to get him into the gifted program at school. After she jumped through all the bureaucratic hoops, she then had the problem of Brad's procrastinating tendencies and his refusal to go to school. He'd get behind because he'd put his school assignments off until the last minute. So on this particular Monday morning, Brad was refusing to go to school because he still hadn't finished his school project.

On Friday, Anne had called the teacher and the principal, and they agreed to not penalize Brad. He was given until Monday to turn in his project. Brad and Anne had moved to California from New Jersey. Brad's father still lived in New Jersey. So, at times like this, Brad would start saying he wanted to go live with his father. He had said this on this particular morning. Anne alternated between wanting to *scold* him and wanting to *plead* with him. Anne was standing in the doorway to Brad's bedroom. She was about to lose her cool and start yelling, so she S-stopped the dragon in her in its tracks, and she walked away.

She silently yelled, "STOP!" and pictured a big red stop sign. She began to take some slow-deep-belly breaths as she walked away to the living room. She paired her breathing with cools as she inhaled and calms as she exhaled. She repeated to herself a dragon-slaying affirmation: "I AM NOT dependent on Brad obeying me to feel good and be at peace." Then, as she exhaled, she said, "Breathing out calm, I can feel good and be at peace as I allow him to take the consequences of his own actions."

Then Anne imagined *expressing* her stress to Brad. She visualized him and silently began to T-tell herself, "My desire to yell at you is telling me that I hate it that you pull this stunt after I've bent over backwards to get the school officials to help you. And that's because

I'd love it if you'd just meet me halfway. My frustration is telling me that I hate it that you procrastinate and put me in a bind, especially after I have gone out on a limb for you. And that's because I'd love it if you would appreciate my going out on a limb for you and do *your* part to be responsible."

As Anne O-observed the gap between what she would love to have happen and her ability to get it to happen, she noticed a familiar feeling of frustration. She looked through the situation with Brad to see if there was someone in her family growing up that she could express the same feelings to and when. She saw herself as eleven years old. There were two people in her family with whom she felt the same kind of frustration: her brother Ned and her father.

Anne had been forced to be overly responsible after her mother died when Anne was ten, soon to be eleven. Her father started drinking, and she had to get him up to go to work before she went to school. Her brother Ned was struggling in school, and she had to help him with his schoolwork. Like Brad, he put off his assignments until the last minute.

As soon as Anne identified the hidden hurt of feeling frustrated and unappreciated after her mother died, her helplessness faded. She felt empowered. Brad was neither her father nor her brother, and she was not a child. And, although Brad could not see his father as often as he did before the move to California, his father had not died as Anne's mother had. Anne could stop feeling guilty. She could now stop coddling Brad as she had her father and brother.

Anne then P-proceeded to close the stress gap by lovingly picturing her son and silently saying, "I know in my heart that you would have gotten things done on time if you could've, but you couldn't in this situation so you didn't." .Anne then proceeded to coolly and calmly walk back to Brad's room. She was firm and decisive. No manipulating. No pleading. No impotent yelling.

Anne proceeded to do the four steps of L-O-V-E: the left hand/right hand technique. She related to Brad that she understood how he felt. "I know you miss your Dad. And I know it's hard to get your work done on time," she said from her heart with her left hand.

"However," she said from her right hand, "you have to get up right now, or there will be serious consequences. There will be no more football and no more getting to see your friends. The TV will be taken out of your room unless you start to be more responsible with your schoolwork."

Brad could feel the energy of his mother's internal shift. She meant business. She was no longer *confusing* the current situation with the helplessness she felt in the past. Nor was she feeling crippled by her compassion for Brad not having his father close.

Later that day, she called her friend and did some more work with looking through the present situation. She was able to fully face her personal emotional history and cry for the overburdened little girl she had been, who didn't get to mourn her mother's death. She had tried to fill her mother's shoes instead. When Anne first spoke to Brad about his procrastination and refusal to be responsible, she was a helpless young girl. The current stress was reminding her of the knee-buckling stress of having a depressed father and an irresponsible brother to motivate.

* * *

The focus for this week is on practicing using all 8 steps for slaying the dragon. Use the steps in creative ways unique to the stressful situations you are facing. Remember, you can just S-stop and breathe, and then go immediately to doing the left hand/right hand technique of L-O-V-E for conflict.

Later you can do the look through technique as it applies to the specifics of the stressful situation you are confronting. Do the look through alone, with your partner or a friend. Think of yourself as flowing through life like a graceful athlete or dancer. You can fluidly apply the steps.

Remember, the essence of the 8 steps is to stop and love: stop and replace a fear focus with a love focus. This way you can focus on and achieve desired outcomes instead of being hampered by a fear focus that fixates on undesirable outcomes.

Week Ten

Cultivating Happiness

GIVE UP THE HABIT OF FEELING BAD & FOCUS ON FEELING GOOD

SINCE THE RENOWNED PSYCHOLOGIST MARTIN SELIGMAN wrote *Authentic Happiness,* happiness has become the subject of serious scientific study. How we can cultivate happiness and other positive emotions became the goal of a new positive psychology.

This is interesting to me because I always told children that the letters Ph.D. after my name meant that I was a people's happiness doctor; and for adolescents and adults I'd say the letters meant that I was their personal happiness doctor. My job was to help them understand what was making them unhappy so that they could be happy again. Therefore, in addition to cultivating happiness, we need to remove what I discovered was a *basic* fear of being happy.

Why We Develop a Fear of Feeling Good & Being Happy

"Whenever I feel really happy, as I do after I meditate, my son and daughter start acting up and bring me down." Mary was talking about how frustrating it is to stay in a place of peace around her teenagers. What's going on? Somehow her children are fearing a loss. It's as if they are thinking, "Where is Mommy? What have you [the happy, peaceful person before them] done with our Mommy?" "How were you when your kids were small?" I asked Mary. "Anxious," she replied. Clearly, the relaxed person was not the mother they were used to, and they felt a loss. They were scared.

Our first source of security is found in our mother's arms. As infants, we can feel her tension and her concern in the cells of our little-baby body. Early in our mother's arms, our brain is developing chemical connections. And we start wiring in our associations of what feels safe. Insofar as our primary caretaker often felt bad— mad, scared, anxious, sad and depressed—we learn to link feeling bad with feeling safe and secure.

The hypothalamus is the seat of emotions. It is the bartender of the brain; early on it starts serving up brain brews associated with safety and security. We can become addicted to the negative emotions exhibited by our primary caretaker, mother, father, grandmother, etcetera. Just as an alcoholic is hooked on his or her beverage of choice, we are hooked on feeling bad in some form.

If your primary caretaker was anxious and angry, you come to associate feeling safe with being anxious and/or angry. You may seek out a partner that is anxious and angry. If your primary caretaker was depressed as well, you can add a dash of depression. Voilá! You have the brain brew that makes up your specific cockeyed cocktail of mother-security. Things can be going well, and you get scared. Your fear may fuel a fight with a loved one so you can get that intoxicating feeling of the negative emotions associated with safety.

There is a protective pattern people develop so as to avoid the pain of loss. It's as if we think, "If I keep my body contracted and tense, then I am prepared for and protected from disappointments. Makes sense. Right? Sure does. But it does interfere with happiness. It is in the nature of the dragon, the reptile brain, to focus on danger so that we can insure our survival. Still, there is another source: our experience with our primary caretaker(s).

Often our parents set an example of indulging the bad habit of playing the blame-game. But even if they didn't, the blame-game comes out of our feeling dependent on others and our environment to feel good and be at peace. The blame-game is just another aspect of the dragon of our dependency and desire. We sling mud at others and at our circumstances for causing our misery. Slinging mud keeps us mired in mud. When we have no power to change our circumstances, blaming is muddy thinking about who we are and what we are capable of accomplishing. The POWS taught us that we have the power to feel good by choosing a love focus instead of a fear or blame focus.

Consider how your mother tended to be. Anxious? Angry? Depressed? All of the above? What did you see on her face most of the time you were growing up? A frown? A smile? Approval? Disapproval? How often did you see her happy? How often did your father seem happy?

Remember that the observer effect in physics can help us break our addictions, especially the one to feeling bad. Once we look under a microscope at the mass of moving electrons, they freeze like deer staring into the headlights of a car. Simply noting and then linking our negative emotions to love, we can break the pattern of being negative. If you practice the 8 steps and the following meditations, you can redirect the archaic chemical aqueducts and rewire the neural pathways in your brain. Feeling good and being happy *can* become the norm, and feeling bad becomes the exception.

Morning Meditation: Cultivating Happiness with a Love Focus

This meditation is a variation of the one found in *Love Conquers Stress*. This one helps you practice returning to the happiness and joy of a love focus when stress strikes. You slay the dragon of dependency and desire by monitoring your motivation. You observe your desires and emotions, *link them to love and let them go.*

• Start doing the following meditation for a few minutes each morning before breakfast. Start with five minutes and work up to twenty. Sit or lie down in a comfortable place. You practice feeling good by keeping yourself free of stress. Learning to be free of the stress hooks helps to foster your health, happiness, and well-being.

• You do not need to tape the meditation and play it back. Just read it over and get the essence of it: you are going to relax and simply watch and listen, see and hear, whatever comes into your awareness. The purpose is to practice keeping yourself cool, calm, and at peace.

You practice identifying and unhooking the stress hooks of your emotions and desires as they arise. If you already meditate and have a mudra (hand position) that you use, then use it. Otherwise simply place your palms in your lap with your left hand cupping your right hand and your thumbs just barely touching.

• Soften your belly and do slow-deep-belly breathing. Breathing in, feel you belly rise. Breathing out, feel your belly fall. Now bring your attention to your breathing. Notice the sensation of the air as you inhale through your nose. Notice the coolness of the air passing over your sensitive nasal membranes. Think the word c-o-o-l as you breathe in. As you exhale, think of how the air has warmed up in your body, and silently say c-a-l-m.

• Send a wave of warmth and heaviness down through your body from your neck, down through your shoulders, chest, abdomen, pelvic region and on down through your legs and out the soles of your feet.

• Now you are ready to begin the heart of the meditation. Identify your stress, anger, fear, sadness, and depression. Using a quieter and calmer version of the shift your focus and energy technique, you identify a negative emotion. You then *link it to love and let it go.* For example, you might say: "Ah, there's my anger over being misunderstood. It tells me that I hate being misunderstood. And that's because I'd love to be understood."

• You may go straight from the negative to the positive and skip using the word hate. For example, you may remember an incident or anticipate something coming up. "Ah, there's my desire for approval telling me I'd love it if everyone always liked me." Or, "Ah, there's my fear that I might forget to go to the store telling me I'd love to remember to go to the store today." As another emotion or issue comes up, you once again link it to love and let it go.

• If you are able to stay with the mantra of c-o-o-l and c-a-l-m with no intruding negative emotions, that's fine. If not, that's fine, too.

Each time a sensation, emotion, thought, memory, concern or issue arises in awareness, you silently say to yourself something like: "Ah, there's my_____. It's telling me I hate or don't like it when_____. And that's because I'd love it if_____." Then return to c-o-o-l and c-a-l-m.

• Recenter your awareness on your breath. Thinking c-o-o-l as you breathe in and c-a-l-m as you breath out. If you prefer, after silently saying c-o-o-l and c-a-l-m a few times to start the meditation, you may choose to simply focus on the sensation of the air coming in and going out of your nostrils.

• When another emotion arises, you identify it, and do the same as before. You *link it back to love and let it go.* You feel good in the face of stress as you just keep linking any negative emotion to love and letting it go. If it comes up again, you do it again. You use the word *my* before the emotions and issues to *own* them psychologically as a truth about your personal emotional history. But you use my in a relaxed, non-grasping way in order to achieve a *neutral* position with regard to all of your emotions, desires, issues and concerns.

• As you go through your day, focus on feeling good by detaching from the dragon by linking your desires and emotions to love and letting them go. Practice being *free* on a moment-to-moment basis.

Evening Meditation: Restoring Happiness by Repenting

Something Christopher Reeve said in an interview after he was confined to a wheelchair really grabbed my attention. He quoted Abe Lincoln as saying,. "When I do good, I feel good. And when I do bad, I feel bad. That is my religion." We do feel good in our heart and soul when we do good. Review your day before going to sleep. "Did I treat others with love, kindness, patience, acceptance, compassion, and empathy? What did I do today that I feel good about? Really relish the good you did. Thank your higher power for helping you. Ask yourself, What do I feel bad about?"

• After you review your day, you'll feel good by *repenting* for the words and actions you regret. Visualize the people you wish you had been more loving and patient with in an empty chair. Express how sorry you are for your words or actions. Then tell the person you wronged what you would have loved to have said and/or done differently. "I'm sorry that I hurt you by saying or doing_____. And I would have loved to have said and/or done_____."

• After you review and repent, you release judgments against others and yourself by using the *mantra of compassion*. When someone attacks you with angry words, it helps to remember that he or she is suffering and resorting to anger to express pain.

Visualize the person and silently say: *"I know in my heart that you would have done differently if you could have done differently but you couldn't so you didn't."* Now extend the mantra to yourself for the words and actions you regret from the day. *"I know in my heart that I would have done differently if I could have done differently but I couldn't so I didn't."* Resolve to speak or act in similar situations in the future with the soul qualities you want to actualize in your life. Notice how good it feels to repent and to resolve to act differently.

Seeding Unconditional-No-Matter-What-Happens Happiness

At the end of *A Simple Path* by Mother Teresa, I found a poem entitled *Anyway*. I felt it was a recipe for slaying the dragon's conditional happiness and achieving unconditional happiness: "my happiness is *not* dependent on anything external." The author of the poem is Kent Keith. His poem consists of ten of what he calls paradoxical commandments. They are discussed in detail in his book *Anyway*. For our purposes here, I have selected four of them.

In essence, you do good for its own sake because doing good makes you feel good. Don't do good for approval, prestige, power, money, and/or admiration. Notice how practicing these commandments puts your focus on feeling good *now*, not later.

State the affirmations I added. They can help you seed your day with the joy of unconditional-no-matter-what-happens happiness.

> • *People are illogical, unreasonable, and self-centered.*
> *Love them anyway.*

[Today, I AM going to love others no matter what they do!]

> • *If you do good, people will accuse you of selfish, ulterior motives.*
> *Do good anyway.*

[Today, I AM going to do good no matter what others think!]

> • *The good you do today will be forgotten tomorrow.*
> *Do good anyway.*

[Today, I AM going to do good because it makes me feel good now!]

> • *People really need help but may attack you if you help them.*
> *Help people anyway.*

[Today, I AM going to help others not for recognition or reward, but because I feel happy when I help ease the pain of others!]

* * *

The focus for this week is on getting comfortable with being happy and feeling good. Practice the meditations. Identify when you are lapsing into the old habit of feeling bad.

Stop the blame game. Remember that when you blame others for *making* you feel bad, you make your happiness dependent on what they say and do. Your happiness is dependent on you and what you *focus* on. Unconditional-no-matter-what-happens happiness is the goal. And it is a supreme spiritual and psychological achievement.

Remember, being negative is a way to protect ourselves from the pain of loss and disappointment. Eventually, we lose everyone and everything we love. So what do we do? We deny this fact. The truth is we suffer because we love, and this is unavoidable.

At the same time, we suffer more because we focus on feeling bad instead of feeling good. This is something we can avoid by learning how to replace a fear focus and a loss focus with a focus on feeling good and being happy. I once heard Dr. Wayne Dyer make the profound statement that feeling good is feeling God. He referenced the fact that the ancient Celtic word for *good* is God.

Epilogue

Saint George & the Dragon

THE SYMBOLISM OF SAINT GEORGE BATTLING THE DRAGON

According to the legend of Saint George and the dragon, Saint George slew the dragon and saved the princess Sabra "with the help of Christ." Aside from the literal understanding that Jesus appeared to help George, what can the slaying of the dragon by the power of Christ symbolize for the inner psychological and spiritual life of everyone? What does the power of Christ mean as a fundamental human experience no matter whether you are Christian, Buddhist, Muslim, etcetera, or profess no religion at all?

The power of Christ points to the power of love. The core of Christ's teaching involves love and forgiveness. He taught us to "love thy neighbor as thyself." The dragon in us desires to receive for the self alone. This is the core of what the Kabbalah calls the Evil Inclination. And the essence of all 8 steps is to replace a selfish, reactive fear focus with a love focus that honors self and others.

Shifting to a love focus involves focusing on loving and accepting others as they are instead of trying to change them. In effect, we slay the dragon in us with the sharp-focused awareness that is our sword of love. This is the love focus fostered by the four inner steps and extended to others in the four outer steps. With the four outer steps conflict becomes a dance of love instead of a battle of fear and anger.

The princess saved by Saint George is our innermost heart, our very soul, where love, the ultimate power in the universe, resides. By slaying the dragon, we release our capacity to love freely without the sticky fingers of trying to control others. We realize that our feeling good and being at peace do not depend on anything external to ourselves. When we take the letter x out of external, we have the word eternal. What is eternal is not the stuff of the world but the stuff of our heart: love—the energy animating all of life.

After finishing the above paragraphs, I took a break and went to dinner. When I returned I turned on the TV and found a black-and-white romantic comedy from 1945 was in progress: *Her Highness & the Bellboy*, starring Hedy Lamarr. The scene I was watching involved the bellboy reading a story to a small group. The story was about a boy, a princess, and a dragon.

The boy in the story decided that he would save the princess from the dragon by offering himself up for the dragon to eat. He wanted to set the princess free to marry a prince. By his gesture, he hoped to prove to the princess how much he loved her.

The dragon appears. The boy told the princess to run. He then walked up to the dragon. The dragon had teeth "as sharp as swords" and "a tail that could knock over a castle."

The boy faced the dragon and laughed. The dragon was startled and turned pale. "You're not afraid of me?," the dragon asked.

"No. I'm not afraid of you!" the boy bellowed. And with that the dragon started to shrink.

"Not even a little?" asked the dragon.

"Not at all," said the boy. And the dragon got even smaller.

The boy then said, "You're only a caterpillar to me." The dragon shrunk and became a caterpillar.

The princess appeared by the boy's side. "Why didn't you run when the dragon appeared?" he asked.

"Because I'd rather be eaten by a dragon with you than marry a prince," replied the princess.

"But I am not a prince," the boy said. She agreed that he was not a prince by title, but that he was a prince in his heart. For her, what was in his heart was more important than anything else.

They married and lived happily ever after. Now, when you see a caterpillar, know that you are seeing what was once a dragon.

The bellboy tells us, "The moral of the story is that fear makes things large. Courage makes things small." As always, I was stunned by the synchronicity of this story. I was finishing this book on how to slay the dragon, and I just happen to turn on a movie where a man is reading a story about a dragon. For me, the important message is that many of our fears stem from when we were small and helpless children. So often current circumstances unconsciously remind us of when we were small and helpless. But when we have the courage to look through the hidden hurts of our past, we transform our fear, the scary dragon, into a caterpillar. The dragon is really a caterpillar, symbolizing the clingy, dependent child in us as opposed to a butterfly, symbolizing our capacity to love freely.

The Kabbalah tells us that the solid appearance world of ordinary reality is the one-percent reality, and the invisible spiritual realm is the ninety-nine-percent reality. From the perspective of our small human ego, the appearance world seems large and real. But from the perspective of our sacred spiritual self, the spirit of God within us, the appearance world is small. I find that as soon as I get sucked back into giving power to the fears spawned by a focus on material reality, the daily dialogue with the Divine reminds me of my error.

I was given a big message about the appearance world just the other day when I was in New York City at what appeared to be a little, hole-in-the-wall donut shop. The owner was from Trinidad. He proudly proclaimed that his jelly donuts had organic strawberry jelly from Italy. There was jelly in every bite as it was evenly distributed. The tiny shop with only two stools and a small counter was deceiving: the donuts were incredibly delicious. I felt like I was Homer Simpson, and I had died and gone to donut heaven. But more than that, the owner was a wise man.

"Why are people so angry?" the owner asked, after learning of my background in psychology. My first thought was because we identify with our body and not our spirit and soul. Instead of saying that, I gave a social and psychological explanation involving the breakdown of the family. When I finished, he said, "I think it is because we identify with our body, and with where we live. I'm from America. I'm from Europe. I'm better than you." He said what I'd thought but censored. The Divine had spoken through him.

Appendix

Overview of the 8 Steps

THE FOLLOWING IS A SUMMARY of the 8 steps to love and three techniques excerpted from *8 Steps to Love*. The four inner steps spell the acronym STOP and the four outer steps spell the acronym LOVE. These two words are a meta-message: STOP the stress and replace it with LOVE. They become a kind of conditioned response, a reminder or affirmation to trigger you to RELAX and, in the case of the stress of conflict, LISTEN.

Remember, with the first four steps you shift your from a fear focus to a love focus so you can feel better and be more effective. And with four outer steps, you help the person you are listening to shift from a fear focus to a love focus so he or she can feel better and be more effective in dealing with stress.

The Four Inner Steps to Love When Stress Strikes

S–Stop the dragon within you in its tracks by using the sharp focused awareness that is your sword of love. You notice a stress signal (you are tense, nervous, upset and/or straining to be understood); then silently shout "STOP!" Then smile inwardly as you take a slow deep breath. Focus on sensations of cool air entering your nostrils and spreading through your nose and into your head giving you a cool, clear head so you can think clearly. As you do belly breathing, silently state with total self-assurance: "Breathing in cool, I stop and still my mind and, breathing out calm, I stop and still my body. Breathing in, I can keep my mind cool and, breathing out, my body calm no matter what!" Take slow deep belly breaths and silently tell yourself "cool" as you breathe in while feeling sensations of cool air spreading through mind so you can think clearly. And, as the air has warmed up in your body, imagine sensations of warmth and heaviness spreading throughout your body and tell yourself "c-a-a-l-m-m" as you breathe out.

T–Tell yourself, "My anger, fear, or sadness is telling me that I hate it when___. And that's because I'd love it if___." Keep doing this—*the shift your focus and energy technique* (page 134 of *8 Steps to Love*). Remember to live from your HEART is to HEAR and feel with your heart what your negative emotion is "T" telling you about what you hate and would love instead.

O–Observe and face the truth of the gap between what you would love to have happen and your ability to attain it. Coolly and calmly determine what, if anything, you can do to attain what you would love to have happen. If what you are feeling is a repeated relationship stress, one that is more intense than is warranted by the situation, then, as you fully feel your negative feelings, you open the door to the hidden hurts of the past and do *the look through technique* (page 172 of *8 Steps to Love*). See who it is in your past you could say the same thing to and trust what comes. Heal the hidden hurt and return to the present with firm resolve.

P–Proceed with the peaceful power of pure love to do all you can to close the gap between what you would love and your ability to attain it. Breathing in, ask yourself, "Is there anything else I can do to close the gap?" Pause, then, addressing your higher power breathe out and say, "If not, then I let go and let *You* take over."

If you are still upset, then pray to your higher power. Breathing in silently say, "Please help me see this situation in a new light so I can," breathing out, "let go of my pain (anger, fear, depression), feel better, find peace and resolution." You can also use a variation of the serenity prayer. Breathing in, addressing your higher power, "Please help me accept what I can't change and change what I can." Then breathing out, say, "And please help me know the difference."

Then the key is to relax, watch and listen to what comes. We need to HEAR and feel with our heart what the synchronicity is "T" telling us. If you are facing a conflict then proceed with the peaceful power of pure love to apply the four outer steps to love.

The Four Outer Steps to Love for the Stress of Conflict

L–Listen with love to HEAR and feel with your heart what the other person's negative emotions tell you about what upsets him or her.

O–Open your mind and heart to the other's point of view and what he or she is saying. You are not agreeing—you are just being open.

V–Validate by verbalizing with empathy what you understand the other to be saying about what upsets him or her and what he or she would love to have happen instead. You might say: "You're saying you feel upset or hate it that ____. And that's because you would love it if____." You help the person shift to love.

E–Express with empathy from the peaceful power of pure love in your heart using personal language, e.g., "I feel upset that or I hate it when____. And that's because I would love it if or when____." You shift your focus and energy from what you don't want or hate to what you do want or would love to have happen in the situation.

Return to Love: Shift Your Focus & Energy Technique

Note: It is important to express love with the SAME *or* MORE INTENSITY *with which you feel your negative emotions. Exaggerate the movements to really reach into your heart as if to grab your negative emotions and then shift, lift and return them to love. Remember, you are redeeming the reptile, the dragon, your lower nature with your higher loving nature as you* HEAR *and feel with your heart what your negative emotions are "T"– TELLING you. As you open your fists imagine releasing the butterfly of love, your capacity to love freely without clinging like the caterpillar.*

1. Make a fist with both hands and pull them to your heart. Round your shoulders. Tighten your body and squat down slightly as you

say: Breathing in, my feeling bad (or my anger, fear, sadness, or depression) is telling me that I hate it when, breathing out (fill in the blank)_____. (Refer to something specific such as what someone SAYS or DOES or a certain situation.)

2. Now open your hands. Expand your chest. Stand up straight and as you extend your arms over your head, as if reaching for the sky, say:

Breathing in, and that's because I love it when, breathing out (fill in the blank) _____.

Note: Nature abhors a vacuum so that when you fully express your anger, fear, and sadness, you empty your heart and make room for love to flow.

Reconnecting to Love Lost: Look Through Technique

Let yourself really feel those feelings as though really turning up a flame under the feelings. While really feeling the feelings, quickly: *Look through this person and see who it is in your family you could say those same words to when you were growing up, someone with whom you have felt the same feelings. Trust what comes. How old are you?* You go back to where you lost a love focus to a fear focus.

When you see the person and the scene then *encourage* the child you once were to express what you could not express then. Feel the safety and support of the adult you behind the child you. Now, using the shift your focus and energy technique, focus on what you didn't like and put it in the strong terms of hate. Then state it in terms of what you would love or would have loved instead. For example, imagine telling someone important to you: "I hate it when you yell at me. And that's because I love it when you tell me respectfully what upsets you." Now look through them and see the person in your family when you were growing up to whom you could say those same words and trust what comes. Say the words to this person, knowing you have the backing and support of the adult you to express yourself fully. Modify the words to what the child you would say. Keep it simple. For example, "I hate it when you yell at me and that's because I love it when you talk to me." Do one *I hate it* to one *I love it*. For example, "I hate it when you hit me. And that's because, I love it when you hold me."

Once the child you is finished, visualize hugging that child you back into your heart. Then come back to the present with the heart and soul of that child you now fully in your heart and make your emotional declaration of independence. In the above example, the person could visualize saying, "I deserve to be seen and heard and I will not settle for less than I deserve." Self-esteem is restored and you feel whole.

Eventually, you will be able to make the shift from negative emotions to love without having to go into the *hate* or of having to *relive* past hurts. You simply see the hurts as they arise and the stress will *dissolve*. For example, you'll be able to say: "There's my past hurt over feeling left out." You'll either take steps to be included or decide it's not important.

Love-in-Action: Left Hand/Right Hand Technique

Left Hand (LOV)	Right Hand (E)
Loving, Honoring and Respecting Others	Loving, Honoring and Respecting Yourself
• You feel upset that___.	• And I feel upset that___.
• You would love it if___.	• And I would love it if___.
• For you___.	• And for me___.
• To you___.	• And to me___.
• You hate it that___. And that's because you would love it if___.	• And I hate it that___. And that's because I would love it if___.

These steps are to be used like training wheels on a bicycle. As you practice them and learn to regain your emotional balance, you can eventually discard them and pedal on effortlessly. You will be in the spirit of living from love. You will see without much effort what your anger, fear, and sadness are telling you about what you love so you can shift your focus. You will be able to see more quickly how the negative emotions of the person you may be in conflict with relate to love as well.

Acronyms & Key Concepts

• **A-C-E**
How do we deal with the tests of life and find peace? We A-C-E them by remembering that P-peace E-equals A-acceptance, C-compassion, and E-empathy.

• **Express don't repress or aggress your stress!**
The essence of the 8 steps to stress relief is Stress effectiveness Training which is, in effect, Self-Expression Training/ We learn to choose *expression* over *repression* or *aggression*.

• **F-A-C-E: You can't heal what you don't feel!**
We must feel to heal emotionally. F-A-C-E reminds us that we need to FACE the hidden hurts of our personal emotional history by F-feeling the hurts with A-acceptance, C-compassion and E-empathy.

• **HEAR—T** (3 Applications)
1. We first need to HEAR with our heart what our anger, fear, sadness, and depression are "T" telling us so we can "T" transform our fear focus into a love focus and our energy from fear to love.

2. When we do the spiritual step and watch for synchronicity, we need to HEAR with our heart what the synchronicity is "T" telling us. Then we let go of pain, feel better, find peace, and resolution.

3. Then when we practice L-O-V-E, we HEAR with our heart what the other person's anger, fear, sadness, and depression are "T" telling them so that they can "T" transform their fear focus into a love focus.

• **Hidden Hurts of the Past**
The hidden hurts of our early years interfere with our adult happiness. By using the look through technique (the emotional step of

O-observe the stress gap), we can release the hidden hurt, usually a trauma from our childhood or adolescence.

• Personal Emotional History
Our personal emotional history involves the foundation feelings that mark the key emotionally-charged events shaping our personal identity. If we don't face the truth of our personal emotional history we are doomed to repeat it in the present.

• Repeated Relationship Stress
When we take the emotional step and O-observe the stress gap, we may notice we are experiencing an all-too-familiar feeling. This feeling is usually one of anger, fear, anxiety, frustration, or depression. It signifies that the current situation and the person we are facing is unconsciously reminding us of an earlier situation and person. We may feel the helplessness of a small child and not really know it until we look through the current situation and person.

• S-T-O-P & L-O-V-E
This is the acronym for the 8 steps to love. They help you replace a fear focus with a love focus by showing you how to transform negative emotions into the peaceful power of love.

• Stress Defined
Stress is the pressure we feel from the perceived gap between what we would love to have happen in any given situation and our ability to attain what we would love.

• Symbols of Transformation: The Goal of the Four Inner Steps
The first is the *dragon's cave* where we transform the dragon within us into the freedom to focus on what we would love to have happen instead of what we fear will happen. The cave is like the *cocoon* where the *caterpillar* of our dependency that fosters a fear focus is transformed into the *butterfly* of a love focus. The cave is also likened to the ancient alchemist's *laboratory* where the *lead* of our negative emotions are transformed into the *gold* of love. And the cave is like the *shell* of the oyster where the *parasite* of our dependency is transformed into the *pearl* of a richer and fuller life.

About the Author

Dr. Stephen Royal Jackson has been a stress specialist since 1980 when he completed his dissertation on stress and received his doctorate in clinical and child psychology from the University of Virginia.

Late in 1995, Dr. Jackson had a life-changing spiritual experience which led him to leave the clinical practice of psychology a year later. In 1998, he founded SET (Stress Effectiveness Training) for Life Seminars.

Through his writing and seminars, Dr. Jackson is dedicated to helping people all over the world eliminate the needless suffering and senseless evil caused by ineffective ways of handling stress and conflict.

To this end, Dr. Jackson lectures and conducts seminars, and he has often appeared on national television and radio. Since 1995, he has been using a Christian—inspired and guided by the Holy Spirit—form of the deeply relaxing ancient healing art of Reiki. With the healing power of the Holy Spirit working through him, he has helped many people here and abroad find relief from stress and stress-related pain and disease.